THE SILENCE AT THE SONG'S END

Nicholas Heiney

THE SILENCE AT THE SONG'S END

Nicholas Heiney

Edited by

Libby Purves

and

Duncan Wu

SONGSEND BOOKS

First published in 2007 by
Songsend Books

Copyright © 2007 E.M. Purves

Reprinted 2009

A CIP Record for this book is available from
The British Library Cataloguing Data Office

ISBN 978 0 9557085 0 3

Designed and typeset by
Columns Design Ltd
Printed and bound in Great Britain by
TJ International Ltd

CONTENTS

FOREWORD	vii
THE BEGINNINGS	1
THE ATLANTIC VOYAGE	7
TO SEA AGAIN: 'GOD WAS TO WINDWARD'	17
PREPARING FOR THE PACIFIC: AUTUMN 2002	23
THE PACIFIC CROSSING	33
TOWARDS KOREA: THE HARDEST VOYAGE	51
OXFORD	83
TROUBLED	101
BLAST AGAINST THE CRITICS, 2006	105
THE SILENCE AT THE SONG'S END	107
AFTERWORD *by Professor Duncan Wu*	113
… AND A FINAL WORD *by Rose Heiney*	115

... I sing, as I was told,
inside myself.
I sing inside myself
the one wild song, song that whirls
my words around
until a world unfurls

my ship's new sail
I catch the dew and set
a course amongst the ocean curls

The silence at the song's end
Before the next
Is the world

Nicholas Heiney, 2006

FOREWORD

'My goal' wrote my son Nicholas a few days before he died, 'is to write something I could show to somebody'.

The irony is that he already had. In his short lifetime he shared only his acute university essays, a few formal website accounts of his sailing voyages in the Pacific, and a brief exasperated blast against the literary-critical industry, of which he was rapidly tiring in his postgraduate year. The rest of these poems, narratives, philosophical musings and long vivid sea-logs were found in the weeks after his suicide.

He threw nothing away, but showed his work little respect. I found what follows in his notebooks, in desk drawers on crumpled papers, on Post-It notes casually interleaved in books. I transcribed it all and put it in rough chronological order, mainly to help my own understanding of his life and death. It was forensic. As one friend said during that time, I was 'picking my way across the battlefield'. A few passages were terrifying. Others were so startlingly interesting and inspiring that we compiled a booklet to send to friends.

There was no thought of wider publication. We had private family memories, photographs, a memorial to be commissioned, our own way to make through this bereavement. Diaries, especially those which contain clues to an advancing sickness of the mind , are not always fit to be shared with strangers. Nor did we feel inclined to contribute to any debate about suicide, depression and mental illness in young men – important subject though that is. We had, and still have, a sense that Nick was in many ways so untypical of his generation and century that it is hard draw any general conclusions from what happened to him.

That view was confirmed by his psychiatrist, to whom he was frankly 'a puzzle', and by Professor Duncan Wu, who like us finds more answers to the puzzle of Nicholas Heiney's psyche in poetry – particularly of the Romantic period – than one could ever find in psychiatry.

So publication was not a first thought. As everything was typed out, though, it became more and more apparent that although the reclusive nature of his illness and his lifelong extreme perfectionism inhibited him from showing them , the sea-logs and many of the other writings were written to be read. He would casually write 'If you read this ...' or 'I'm sorry, I must go back a day –'. The sense of privateness receded, replaced by a belief that this was, as Professor Wu writes in his afterword, a kind of testament. It records the experiences, terrors, vision and beliefs of a rare and strange spirit, whose joys and despairs both place him closer to mystics and romantics of the past than to the age he was born in.

Moreover, although the first two sea-logs are brief and factually schoolboyish, and included here merely for completeness' sake, his more private account of sailing the Pacific as a deckhand on the square-rigged barque *Europa* at eighteen is too vivid not to share. So are some of the poems and reflections.

Nicholas was a natural mystic; although he never spoke about religion except in mild exasperation at the prejudices of organized churches, we now know that for years his inner world was populated by demons and angels, the spirit and the shine of heaven and the terror and beauty of poetry. His relationship with Shelley's strange 1815 poem 'Alastor', which Professor Wu explains in his afterword, was not something he ever discussed openly. From the age of seventeen his email address was alastor1815@hotmail.com, and the password was 'shelley', but nobody knew how deep that myth went with him.

All this we came to understand in the bewildering, sorrowful months after his death. With caution we shared the documents with other cooler heads, and it is their encouragement which enables us to present Nicholas Heiney's mind and work to you now, adding only enough narrative to give the writings a context. Lovers of the sea will find much in it, I think, and believers in the power of poetry even more. We hesitated a little over adding some earlier material, but the light that it sheds on his mental development seemed to make it worthwhile reproducing even the simpler writings. I have used emails and notes on chronology simply when they serve to link the story together.

With some diffidence, I should say that we are also publishing this for another reason. It seems to us to contain truths and perceptions about life which – although they come from an unusual and troubled soul – have already shown an ability to touch hearts and lives. And we know from what Nicholas said, and from the conscientious way that he worked when he was doing maintenance high aloft on the tall ship *Europa*, that he had a strong and humble sense of wanting to contribute to posterity. On the ship he attended carefully to the seizing and splicing of footropes and handholds high in the rigging, consciously thinking of the security and safe passage of strangers who would come after him . In his writing too there are many handholds. They support us to this day.

None of us can expect more than that: the hope that somewhere up in the crazy cobweb of life we have left a good piece of work which will serve fellow-beings. Despite his youth and the illness which overcame him, Nicholas did leave something worth having. And as he himself wrote:

> What is important is to remember that it is not the way in which we record our existence, but that we do record it. In the air, and everywhere around, we must remember how the streets ring out for every soul that thought and felt and passed through them in weakness and in strength.

LIBBY PURVES
Westleton,
December 2006

THE BEGINNINGS

A short account of Nicholas Heiney's 23-year life seems needed, and this I will provide as dispassionately as a mother can manage. He was born in November 1982, on the rising tide, in the British Hospital for Mothers and Babies at Greenwich. Superstition has it that a baby born when the tide is rising will be a boy. We named him Nicholas merely because we liked the name and it was nearly Christmas, and it was only two decades later that we discovered that St Nicholas of Myra is the patron saint of both sailors and scholars. He was a very alert baby, smiled early and appreciated a joke. One elderly babysitter said 'These clever ones, they're hard work.' And more reflectively: 'What a little bundle of worry!'

His sensitivity showed early, and for him, stressfully. He asked a lot of questions and entertained a lot of fears. When he was four and the great beech tree fell on the end of our house in the 1987 hurricane, he wept because 'I will be dead before it can grow up again so beautiful'. I tried to say no, no … but of course, he was quite right: it was a 200-year-old tree. At four he had grasped ideas of mortality, beyond the comfortable assumptions of daily life. On the other hand he also grasped the solace of language. We wrote a small book together about the tree – 'The Hurricane Tree', still used in schools; and when his sister was hysterical in another storm he came up and said sternly to her 'Rose, do not fear, no stranger comes'. Perfect iambs; proof that Shakespeare caught the natural metre of heightened emotion. He took to poetry early. We had a tape of 'The Night before Christmas' and one day in the car he suddenly recited it, word perfect even in the difficult bits like 'As the moon on the breast of the newfallen snow casts a lustre of midday to objects below'. It taught me a lot about how pre-literacy worked: how people once remembered poems and ballads verbatim so they could pass them on, simply because they mattered so much.

He also demonstrated early a romantic love of the sea. On family trips in our small boat he would creep from his bunk in night-watches, to sit with whichever of us was on the helm and watch the silhouettes of the sails moving across starry skies.

1

Even the gentle local infant school was hard for him: he was always afraid of doing something wrong, and would wail illogically 'we're starting maths tomorrow and I don't know any'. But in the school plays he gained confidence, played good parts and had his first small triumphs. He retained an old-fashioned turn of phrase, prefiguring the almost Victorian language of some of his sea-logs; at seven, asked whether he would do again at assembly a puppet play which he had devised in the playground, he replied formally 'I would be honoured'.

At bigger schools life was more difficult. During his most nervous period, at about nine, he alarmed us and the headteacher by saying that 'even the bricks in the walls are curling themselves up to throw themselves at me'. The image, we now know, remained: there is a terrifying unfinished poem from his late adolescence repeating it. He hated to be teased but with his sense of the terrible solid reality of words, he was shocked at the idea of taunting others back: 'I could say things that would destroy him, but I couldn't.' Eventually he found equilibrium at Royal Hospital School at Holbrook, where he served as a head of Juniors, pastoral and kind to younger children. He had good friends there; but at seventeen, the first year of A levels, he suffered a violent illness of the inner ear – labyrinthitis – which during his slow recovery threw him into an extreme post-viral depression. He fought this in every way possible but it took a toll, and the damage may have contributed to the more serious and terrifying psychosis which it now seems clear was developing when he died. His darker writings begin at this time; and while it would be wrong to reproduce much of the scribbled diary from this period, I offer a few lines which relate clearly forward to the imagery of his later and more accomplished, writings.

I set the date for Saturday the fifth
To give a little time for me to think
About the sound of half-deserted rooms
And streetlamps blocking out the light from stars
Where rolling banks of cloud will not suffice
To shield a man from his own Paradise.
Through winding streets there lurks a nemesis
In stone cold air, in shadows of the night.
I did it anyway
I did it anyway
I will do it again
I will descend into the inky night once more.

Bad Trip

While lying, waiting in the shimmering cold
It was as if the bricks broke free and hurled
themselves with vice to cleanse the sullied world
from me who stood behind perception's bars

as if it were a judgement from the stars
searing through my icy prison bars

But the bricks stayed in still
because they knew with every breath
that every ghostly shuddering chill
was marking time until my death
I lay quite still within my eerie cage
convulsing, contorting and feeling its rage.

Incidentally, the title of that last poem and the violence of the imagery may suggest, to a modern reader, the use of drugs. I think we can rule that out, for several reasons. First because at the time of those writings he had no possible access to them; secondly because he knew early on – from a bad reaction to a prescription drug – that he belonged to the one-in-eight subjects who should keep away from mind-altering substances, because their minds are fragile enough anyway. He was, despite the mysticism, eminently sensible: the strange visions, both lovely and horrible, which beset him all his life and particularly strongly in the last five years did so unprovoked by drugs.

It is also worth pointing out that they did not beset him constantly. He had friends, jokes, sailed regattas and won the occasional prize; he knew elation, sporting effort, ordinary ambition. There are some light poems from this time and some affectionate ones too. He was, for example, vastly amused by the press reports of the 'quarterlife crisis' afflicting prosperous 25-year-olds, and wrote this:

O, what good has become of me
this quarter of a century?
There's no more pleasure, so I'm told
In growing saggy, boring, old
And losing youthful symmetry
O God, what has become of me?

My years now number twenty five
I use my clothes as a disguise
In corduroys and cardigans
My youth is laid to martyrdom.
And a bedtime past eleven
Is exceedingly unwise.

O dear God, will you rescue me,
from middle age and family
Fatherhood and daily hobbies,
Buying cats and dogs and rabbits
Buying two if one is free –
Rescue me from afternoon tea!

Now as my tawdry life proceeds,
Inch by inch, my hairline recedes

3

The loss of youth with looks' renown
Is leaking from my vanishing crown
And my body to age concedes
The mind will lose its youthful needs.

But why have a care about oneself
When twenty-five, and in good health?
Why so ungrateful? Why so sad?
Can middle age be all that bad?

He was doing Physics A level as well as English and History, an odd mixture at first sight; but then, clarity of expression is a pre-requisite for a physicist. And I wonder now, having read his writings, whether the scientific rigour and certainties of physics did not comfort something in him that valued rationality simply because it was always under siege, both from poetry and from the first dark tendrils of psychosis. And only a physicist could have written the lines about death:

What we were, we will become
As we give our heat to the desert sun.

He read Ted Hughes and Sylvia Plath with close attention, and when Frieda, Plath's daughter, was staying with us he sat up half the night with her in the kitchen, deep in analysis of her own poems. His approach to poetry, good or bad, was always one of gentle careful interrogation, trying to understand the mind and intention of the writer rather than evaluating or categorizing it. On the other hand, it is worth stressing that he was emphatically not a 'suicide-groupie' or romanticizer of early death; he knew all too well how irritated Frieda was by the cadre known among us as the 'Plath-loonies' who become unhealthily obsessed with her mother's death.

But after that illness at seventeen the underlying fragility and sense of isolation, of which his family had been aware all his life, began to intensify. He fought it hard. During the period of his illness he remained steadfastly determined to join in Tall Ships 2000, the millennium sea-race across the Atlantic, as a trainee aboard the Dutch square-rigged barque *Europa*. His doctors warned that the illness might have made him dangerously susceptible to seasickness, so he tested himself on a short North Sea crossing aboard the Lowestoft sailing-trawler *Excelsior*. Compared to the strength and lyricism of his later logs his account is brief, but has some vivid moments, expressive of a boy's first times at sea:

Excelsior, 2000.

It is now 8.30. For the second time in my life, I am joining a strange boat as crew. I never know what to say when I first come aboard … 'Hi, I've come to join your boat'? How do they know who the hell I am? I could be some demented stranger who happens to be passing by.

My bunk is on top of some important bloke's bunk so I had better keep my annoying personal habits to a minimum.

The wind is set to make us close-hauled to Rotterdam but if it goes into the South, it will be a beam reach across which would be great.

The Mate on board sailed across the Atlantic with my Mum many years ago, so I shall try and get some stories off him.

I really hope that I can make a good impression upon the crew and not be seasick or wimpish. The name of the bo'sun is Rob, I think.

My first impressions of the boat are of bewilderment. I have never seen anything quite like it. The deck space is huge because it is a fishing-boat. Next to my bunk is a fire bell which you have to turn to operate. This ensures that you will be deafened as well as burned.

The Dutch guy with the grey hair and moustache is called Harry. the real name of the bo'sun is Ben. Ben the Bo'sun.

Get up tomorrow is at 5.30. I should not be up too late but if the rest of the crew is at the pub that is where I shall be. It is all a matter of fitting in with them. I was given supper on board. I had already had supper but, again, I just wanted to fit in with the rest of the crew. I am certainly the youngest on board, which puts me at a disadvantage. Ben is the only one who is near my age. I must make an effort to fit in otherwise the passage will not go well for me. I do not think that the weather will be very good at all for the passage, so it is better to be in the same boat with people who you get on well with.

It is time for me to take my pills now. I hate them because they keep me low. Not being able to drink is a disadvantage to me, because when I am drunk it is one of the few times that I feel at ease with myself and other people.

Watch times: I am with David the mate. On watch 1600–2000 and 0400–0800. On standby 14–16, 20–22, 02–04, 08–10

Tuesday. So … woke up at 0600, late. Set sail shortly afterwards.

The wind is force 4, 5, 6 perhaps.

It is quite rough in the mouth of Harwich harbour and it is currently raining. Skipper says the passage could take two days, who knows.

OK … so it is now 2030. We had some rough weather. I felt quite seasick so I had to lie down.

I am pleased to note that the ship carries the ever vital piece of equipment, a plastic duck. Not even David the mate knows exactly what it is for. It could be to scare off birds but it is more likely to be a mascot.

We were joined by a racing pigeon today. It still has not left and I don't think it intends to. It was badly dehydrated and its shit was green so we gave it some water and some oatmeal and it perked up.

The wind has dropped to virtually nothing now. Ben the bo' sun spilt some of the skipper's new white paint in the fo'c'sle. I helped him drag the stuff out of it so he could sop up the paint , despite feeling sick. I took the helm on watch today. It is odd because the ship does not have a wheel, and the loads on the tiller are very large even in flat seas.

Things seem to indicate an early afternoon arrival.

Wednesday
0400 Started watch
0500 Wind got up and some light appeared
0600 Wind died down again

The fucking stupid pigeon drowned at about 0530. It tried to fly away but it was not strong enough so it tried to fly back to the boat. It missed by about a metre and fell into the water. All we have to remember it by is the shit which it left everywhere.

0800 Had porridge and a chicken sandwich. We are in the middle of all the shipping right now. We should arrive about 1400.

Holland is so damn flat! Some wanker has blocked the toilet. I have just been asleep.

The next time I see what I am seeing now, I will have been 4 weeks at sea and once again be arriving in Holland. The Bo'sun managed to clear up his mess in the fo'c'sle with a scraper earlier.

1300 Have just done the washing up because I felt that I should do it once before leaving the ship. I am about to go up to see where we are. The toilet is still blocked and David is trying to sort it out.

1310 All sail is now lowered and stowed; soon we should be entering the river. Also retracted bowsprit. I must work to improve my seamanship skills and remember to bring a woolly hat along next time.

1400 The date is May 1st now, and I am back at school. As it transpired, the journey downriver was about 15+ miles and it rained. I helmed for 2–3 hours through an industrial hell hole and arrived at Rotterdam 2000 hours.

Rotterdam itself is an unwelcoming hole. I was glad to get home.

THE ATLANTIC VOYAGE

[The short, briefly reported voyage across the North Sea reassured him that the Atlantic passage in the epic Tall Ships 2000 race might be feasible, despite his slow recovery from the illness. Four weeks at sea among strangers in all weathers is not to be undertaken lightly, but he was unpersuadable, adamant that he would go. He wrote letters to sponsors and sold burgers to raise money . In June 2000 he set off for Boston, to sail the first short leg aboard the Russian cadet ship *Mir* and then join *Europa* at Halifax, Nova Scotia. His log at this stage remains factual and brief. *Mir* was in some ways an easy introduction to square-riggers, being large and mainly manned by Russian cadets.]

MIR, Boston towards Halifax

16th

I feel so nervous that I am sick to my stomach. Breakfast consisted of some greasy meat and soda bread. It was not too bad.
1140 Set off
1220 Had lunch. Seemed to consist of beetroot soup and some beef-stew-like stuff.
Tea is at 1530

The weather is foggy but quite calm at the moment. The wind is in the wrong direction. Helm watch & lookout watch from 1600–1700 daily. Pantry duty: 1100 Monday 17/7. The cupboards in my cabin are tied together with bale string.

1645 Had conversation with Ray [fellow-trainee from Boston]. 'Have you seen the food around here? I couldn't eat the bread even. How the fuck can they fuck up peas? Lucky I brought my supplies of Noodles and nutty butties along with me. If you cain't look at it, you cain't eat it, I say!'
    To be fair, the meal was smoked haddock, uncooked peas and soda bread.

17th

0400 Watch. The crew were not really interested in teaching us anything. Helped to make some anti-chafe things but that was all. Fog has lifted a little.

1215 Have just done Pantry duty. Not much to it really. I just laid a few tables and that was it.

2040 No wind right now but it should fill in soon, we do not know where from but it should be around 20 knots. Went up lower futtock shrouds today. It was good fun and I did not feel nervous, much. Shower 2030.

18th.
Last night's watch was the quietest ever. Did nothing. Slept from 0830 to 1200. Either the food is getting better or I am getting used to it.

The weather is still very slight but there is just enough wind to keep the sails full. We are surrounded by fog once more. I am on cabin (Kubrik) cleaning duty on Thursday, so full sail ahead so I do not have to do it.

2000 Wind has picked up nicely. It is very foggy but the ship is moving along beautifully now. Some people were singing with a guitar earlier. The ship has woken up.

19th
2000 Wind is now at gale force. We cannot get a pilot until 0900 tomorrow. I went out on the bowsprit – pretty wild and scary. The bowsprit was bucking up and down madly with the waves, and despite the height, spray soaked us at regular intervals. Getting out on the bowsprit when wet feels like tight-rope walking on a moving rope. The wind seems to suck the air out of your lungs.

[In Halifax he joined the 150-ft Dutch barque Europa, a favourite of the tall ships fleet. Converted after her beginnings as a lightship into a sailing ship with a series of international crew, she circles the world from Europe to the Antarctic doing charter, training and racing voyages. The small permanent crew on this occasion (a crew he later joined for six months in the Pacific) were supplemented by thirty-odd young trainees between 16 and 25, of whom he was one.]

Europa Transatlantic: Boston–Amsterdam

Sunday: v. apprehensive. I am in C Watch. First trainee briefing: the first rule is not to feed the Captain's dog Gander. The second is not to turn up drunk on watch. We then did two hours of training in which we were shown how to work with the ropes on board and how to go aloft. My mind was numbed during this whole briefing, in sheer terror of what I was about to embark on.

Monday. Day of departure.

Was woken at 0400 for cleaning for 2 hours and I am on watch at 0800, shitty luck.

Departed 0845 to the sound of cheering crowds and foghorns. The sails are now set but are backing as we approach the start line. At the moment, I see this whole crossing as more of an overall concept rather than something that is actually happening to me. At some point I will try to get some sleep. I am trying to eat because I feel that I should, but my stomach is knotted up with fear, so it is difficult. I am so afraid right now that I think that I will start to cry soon. Some people are very sure of themselves but I am not. 4 weeks at sea is a very very long time.

2000 Wind has filled in a little. We are heading about 140 degrees to get south of the ice and into the Gulf Stream again. I have been shown now how to do bow-watch and which ropes do certain tasks. It is a lot of information but I should get the hang of it.

Tuesday 24 hours at sea, 25th.

0800 Have just come off watch. I had my first bread-baking experience then an hour's bow watch with another guy. Right now I am quite happy just to listen to other people's stories. I don't need to tell all of my own yet. I then scrubbed the decks and came off watch. I must be on deck again at 0900 for some more work.

1320 Have had a lesson on the setting and striking of squaresails. I understand them a lot better, I think. I have now been aloft to the level of the upper topgallants.

26th Weds, 48 hours at sea

Did 0000–0400 watch. It is the worst watch because there is not much time to sleep at either end. During this watch I cleaned the deckhouse to the sound of Greenday. We also heard the sounds of whales and dolphins throughout the night.

1630 Saw many whales and dolphins today. Then did a few hours maintenance on the bowsprit. Today has been hard because I am also tired.

27th Thursday, 72 hours at sea.

Last night's watch was fairly uneventful. I did helm for a while and lookout for a while. A small black bird landed on deck in the night. It could not fly so we gave it some bread and water. I do not know what is happening to it right now.

1200 Quite a good breeze but it is still coming from the East. I really wish that we could get some fair winds because this lack of proper progress we are making is really demoralizing at this early stage in the crossing.

2015 Wind has still risen. It is raining also. I went aloft twice to work on sails in this watch. The Upper staysails and the skysails and t'gallants have been struck.

29th 120 hours at sea. Gale

[Early in the gale, N was elected leader of his watch]

1915 In the gale, a lot of people felt ill, we ripped the main staysail and the foremast lower t'gallant. It was pretty rough with the decks awash. Working aloft was also tough going. My task of watch leader was difficult due to all the absentees. A lot of people were just plain fucking lazy. The gale has subsided now and we are left slopping around for the moment. Who knows what the wind will do next.

30th 140 hours at sea

Wind has become fair now. It is shower day so everybody has clean hair. We managed to break a stunsail beam today; wind seems to be steadily increasing at the moment.

31st 168 hours at sea.

One week! The weather is beautiful . The boat is travelling along well. We are now close to (if not into) the Gulf Stream.

2nd 9 days at sea

The last few days have seen good, fair weather. We are now past our waypoint and are trying to stay south to catch the next depression. Last night was a really beautiful one. Today and yesterday I have been very busy with maintenance. I scrubbed and oiled the shrouds for long periods. Today I went aloft to work on the skysail yard for the first time. The Jacob's ladder is the worst part of it in a big sea, by far.

3rd 10 days at sea!!

Worked on the skysail for 2 and a half hours today. Sea was rolling and it started to rain. I found it extremely tough and tiring. I felt oddly wimpish when I came down.

At this rate we will never reach Amsterdam but I am not too bothered about it at the moment, we will just have to keep plugging forward.

5th 12 days at sea

For the last 2 days we have had lovely weather and are currently flying all of our stunsails. We passed very close to the *Oosterschelde* yesterday and I got some pictures of her.

Today was Harry's birthday. There was a happy hour in the bar and it was all decorated. Some of the boats seem to have nearly finished the race but there is no wind near to the Channel so they are stuck. We still have a long way to go.

I have started drinking now. It was getting too difficult not to.

I am existing in a fairly mindless routine and not giving much thought to anything or worrying too much.

6th 13 days

Disaster today as the grey-water tank broke and grey water came up through the shower drains. It stank the whole boat out and it took a long time to clean out the cabins. Many beautiful dolphin sightings.

15 days at sea

Today I went up to overhaul buntlines. I felt very Newbyish when I was doing it. I also went up yesterday to help set the stunsails.

9th. 16 days at sea 1000 miles from the finishing line.

10th 17 days at sea

Today we flew 30 sails although some of them were not much more than handkerchiefs. We did sustained speeds of 9 knots and the sea was nice and flat. It was a good day but the wind died away at the end and left the boat wallowing.

14th 21 days, 3 weeks at sea

Crossed waypoint at 1600 approx. Sailing along beautifully at 1715 with maintenance in full swing. With about 200 miles to go to the finish, we are still not in sight of land even from aloft (I checked). there is also no mobile phone network yet but I do not expect one really at all until we get very close to land.

Already the ship is looking much better and brighter for all the paintwork that is being done on her. Last night in the skipper's meeting Klaas said that we will continue sailing after the finish line because 'We are a sailing ship'. This sums up the attitude of the captain very well indeed. He is a very good skipper. The best that I have sailed with.

15th 22 days at sea

1400 Land is clearly visible now but I have a mobile phone signal at the moment, however my Parents seem to be away. Never mind. I left a message on their answering machine so they know where I am if they check their messages.

16th 23 days at sea

We expect to arrive at Ramsgate at 0000 tonight. We finished the race at 0039 BST last night. I got to helm over the finish.

[Nick arrived at Ramsgate, went briefly ashore but preferred, he said , to go back to the ship and tidy up. His official account to his sponsors describes the ending:]

It was about 0100 by the time we moored up, and we all ceremonially went ashore for a kebab. We only had 24 hours in Ramsgate, but I still did not feel much like going ashore. I had become too accustomed to the sea and felt a bit bewildered.

On Wednesday 23rd August we set off to Ijmuiden in preparation for the big Parade of Sail to Amsterdam along the wide canal. I don't think I have ever seen so many boats of all sizes on one piece of water. The banks were lined with people for the whole 20 km, and the canal was jammed with carnival boats and private ones. Europa had 80 guests on board and a group of drummers, which gave her a party atmosphere all through the parade. We were at our berth at about one o'clock.

[He met us in Amsterdam, at the climax of the great millennium festival, riding up the long canal amid the press of boats, perched on a high yardarm of *Europa*. Although the preceding log is still bare and factual – largely a preparation for the public log which his sponsors asked for – it is clear from poems and journals that the experience went deep, and that as he continued reading avidly at school, it chimed with the lyrical and romantic insights which connected him to Shelley's story of 'Alastor', of the poet led onward on a voyage that never ended.

His reluctance to leave the ship is characteristic. After the experience, and whatever unrecorded spiritual effect it had on him, it was clear that he found the world of school very difficult indeed to return to. A number of irritable poems ensue, and some more disturbing reflections. He was now just eighteen.]

Youth

All I know about truth
Is its absence in youth.
Youth is a shiny bowl
Holding a million empty souls
We see others but we do not look
We are the empty pages of a ruined book.

Blinded by emptiness in a club
Conformity is a powerful drug
The rope of opinions kills us together
The looks of others are our tether.
Drowning in company's ocean deep
Empty in a dreamless sleep.
The shiny celebration of self
Through clothes and unearned wealth
Is comfort sweet and sickly honey.
We celebrate being slaves to money.
We do not know what we are for,
So we fight youth's hopeless war.

C of E

The walls, the books
The righteous crooks
With guilt to steal their fee
With the brutish rape and torture
Of the Holy Trinity

The church, the charms,
The chanting psalms
Perhaps the church has missed
The strength of every living God
In every Atheist?

The priest, his spells,
The threats of hell
Perhaps he would do well
If he saw that Jacob's ladder
Is a ladder down to hell?

The book, the wealth
On the dusty shelf
Tells us of our fate
The monster stays in his castle
While the man remains at the gate

A Levels

Wooden eyes
Biting skin
Pinpricked skies
Void within,
Purple haze
Fiery drops
Evil maze
Burnt out copse.
Growing thoughts
Winding stalks
Nightmares fought
Rotting corpse.
Caffeine storm
Beating brain
Pure heart torn,
Torn again.

Living under constant pressure, we grow fat. Cottonwool is pulled over my eyes and the exam straps are tightened.

I have led a life of non-achievement. I have no skills. Few friends. How much courage do I need? What is stopping me? I could do it. I must do it. I loathe everything I write and yet it is all that I want to do. I am hideously ugly, outside and in. The noose? The knife? The life?

A levels finish today. The bubble closes and tonight I shall play with insomnia as a suicide plays with a knife.

There is something rotten within me. I know this, because I see it everywhere. My rottenness is in the world around me. It is in the places I carry back and forth. 18 years old and abnormal. I feel as if I hang onto my sanity just barely. Two people are constantly fighting inside me. The characters are fighting in the imaginary world where objects cast the shadows that form reality. I stand just inches away from my own voice, slowly deteriorating as my dreams lose perspective, slide away like light inside a prism and disappear. Ambitions subdued , stewing in my own inadequacy.

It is the voiceless void which fills the empty mind. The last outlet for a waning creativity. On the abyss of eternity, something so finite the walls around me suck in slightly, sensing limitation.

I could tear my character in two, Nick and Alastor, one mild mannered, one a demon.

14

To Stop

To stop and think
(It makes one shrink)
That life is one long trek
And we are lost in laptops and still have not found yet
The secret to our happiness
In a search on the internet
Or the key to our true spiritual home
Or the reason for our love and hate
In the ringtone of our mobile phone
Or in Windows 98.
But now I hear the world's clock chime
And Earth's barman quietly calling time.

It seems to me that history
Has this age forgotten.
Lost in laptops, deadlines, train times and speeding fines
Our souls have become rotten
And as the cities of the ancient world, we gradually decline
Now even in the idle hours
False fantasy TV devours
Us in sex and glamour-crime
Therefore, indeed, we have no need
For any poetic line.

[Such storms once passed, there was by contrast a sense that the world would open up once school was over, and some tenderness for his fellows:]

For the Leavers

When autumn's quiet and weary days are through
and I have travelled far and wide
embraced the world, cast fear aside,
Seen hell amongst the city skies
and heaven in the morning dew
So count myself now blest and wise,
Dear heart, I will return to you.

When night gives way to summer's dawn
And watchful stars to foreign lands have flown
When silver clouds deliver swirling storms
And God will look on me alone
To conquer Hell's e'er lasting storm
I shall be wise, I shall be true
Dear heart, I will return to you

TO SEA AGAIN:
'GOD WAS TO WINDWARD'

[During the autumn before A levels Nicholas applied to Oxford, got an interview, and came back exalted. 'Mum, I need to be taught by those guys. ... ' They turned him down; he resolved to try again, equipped with an encyclopaedic reading list given to him – albeit with no promises – by the senior tutor, Michael Gearin-Tosh. Waiting for A level results, it was time to go to sea again to clear the mists. The sea, as he later wrote, provided him with a peace he found nowhere else.]

My first experience of tallship sailing was on the British schooner, the *Malcolm Miller*. The memory of boarding the ship for the first time, seeing the cramped bunks, and being told that this is also where all meals are eaten, remains with me. I remember particularly being told by the mate, with a definite hint of enthusiasm, that we were living under conditions which commercial mariners refused to live in 60 years ago.

Since this time, I have endured and enjoyed various accommodations. The reason for my original mention of this is that, in my experience, when asking someone about their sailing trip the first thing they will mention is the accommodation. This is generally because when sailing, especially in rough conditions, one forms such a bond with the cramped, untidy living space that it becomes almost a fantasy. On long, hard seawatches I have often fallen into a wild reverie at the very thought of bruising my shins while wrestling to get into my hammock. A major part of the tallship magic is its ability to turn what is effectively an uninhabitable environment into heaven on earth. Whatever the accommodation, whether basic or lavish, I can guarantee some of the best nights' sleep that ever can be had.

[He did not, however, opt to go back to his friends on *Europa* that summer, saying that he should experience an even bigger square-rigger, another nationality of strangers and another way of sailing. He chose the 250 ft Norwegian ship *Christian Radich*, and joined at Antwerp for the 500-mile race to Aalesund in Norway, with his friend Jim. It was on this voyage that the poetic impetus accelerated, and began to be consciously related to the seagoing experience.]

Friday July 6th

Imagination is my absent curse
And so it is that time of year again
To go to sea, for better or for worse
Where silver sails break sun in golden shards
And I can work at being pure again.

The heady rush of middle England's crush
The bars and awkward social teenage circles
Will dissolve into an absent thought
And I can be pure again.

For now my mind is wrapped in cottonwool.
I hope that there is inspiration in the waves.

It is a freer life of limitations. Sailing is not an imprisoning freedom, unlike the freedom given to me here. The sea does not create expectations or demand them.

July 8th.

So it is the first day. Yesterday I was shown to my hammock. Possibly the most uncomfortable night of my life. Strange gushing sounds could be heard on deck and the drunken return of my shipmates did not assist.

1240 Encountered dry Norwegian sense of humour. Had tour of the ship but the best is yet to come.

9th Watches were cancelled last night and began at 1200 with our watch.

Jim had a very bad night, after much swearing, moving from his hammock to a convenient spare bunk.

Rig training began at 0800, at sea before the start at 1100. I made it up to take the gaskets off the royal sail. The rig is far easier to climb than the *Europa* since everything is larger and easier to fit your feet into.

Jim only made it to the bottom of the futtock shroud. I empathise with this mental barrier which he must face. Nothing physical stands in the way: just the very idea of an overhang.

The bosun appears to be the same as many bosuns – loud and authoritative.

The first watch gave me no specific duties apart from the constant re-trimming of sails in order to take the wind up and overtake the *Quatermant*. Everybody is still slightly awkward on board. Ropes attract people like dust, not being quite sure what to do with themselves. In the sail-hoisting, the deck became a snakepit of ropes

18

which were hung and subsequently undone in one of the re-trims.

A first occurred today in the captain's briefing. As we were overtaking the *Staatsraad Lehmkuhl* (of the same handicap) we were instructed to use *more* water! Captain wants us to shed the weight to make us faster.

After the watch (just before writing this) I went aloft with Jim. After much trying we could not quite get him over the first futtock shroud. I know that he will make it. He will not let himself not make it.

I then continued to go aloft to the level of the royal yard. Going aloft is to me a magical experience of which I do not believe I will ever tire. On the way up you are encapsulated in a world of rope, tar, and billowing sails. Height is not an issue since the distance travelled is less important than the over-tarred rung in which a foot must be jammed. Every ratline, shroud and futtock contains the fear, relief and exultation of everybody who has climbed it.

You are ascending through clouds, through your own effort, not the will of any power or God. Yourself, in control and washed clean of identity, association. The mind is drawn to the climb through the jungle of rigging.

When I reach the top of the jungle, the cloudy sails and everything else lie below. I am open to the sky and can look down upon the ship as a soul in heaven looks down upon the earth. Through jungles of complication and stress, to the open sea and sky. Every thought wiped clean, every emotion intensified, every colour brighter.

Day started well at 0000. We sustained 11–12 knots, surfing down the rolling waves in perfect trim. Passing close to an oil rig at night, the sails silvered in the moonlight, contrasting with the garish Gothic firestack. It was an eerie experience.

From 1100 onwards, it has been a dreadful day. Light winds, showers and fire alarms formed the physical symptoms. The sullen wakeup which I received left me fatigued and docile for the watch. People's stares and yells were seemingly directed just for me. Everywhere I stand I am somehow in the way. My fuse grows ever shorter. I never seem to be in the right place at the right time. I watch, I pull, I coil but I do not paint, steer or climb. I feel that the watch leader does not like me very much at all. Social interaction on my part has also been difficult. The cotton wool has returned. I am back in my classroom, awkward and hunched. Every thought passive, every event internalized. What happens next, I do not know.

12th

I write a little later than usual today. Excuse me, three guys dressed in drysuits have just walked by. They must have come from the speedboats. Back in a minute.

As I was saying, I write a little later than usual today. I have been scrubbing my hair in the shower for 20 minutes, attempting to get the white paint out of it. I now make a note to myself to avoid painting whenever possible. 1 litre of paint on target is 2 litres on the deck. This did not please Eyof. A lot of time was spent scrubbing after this incident. Look back and laugh.

Friday 13th

Shortly after this time yesterday, the wind blew up to a force 6–7 by 2230. The first I noticed of this was when I looked up from my book to find the cabin at a slight heel. As the wind strength increased, so did my curiosity, to the point when I could not settle in my hammock. The restfulness of the banjer [accommodation] contrasted with the frantic activity on deck. Sails being struck and the rigging of safety ropes foretold a difficult night.

I find that as soon as the weather shows signs of getting rough, a mental separation occurs between the deck and the cabin. Before, one can wander on deck and in the cabin, vaguely noticing the different atmosphere. When the weather becomes rough, the two are a million miles from each other: one the wet, cold wilderness of lashing ropes and raised voices, where biting cold skin and watery eyes flock onto the ropes and foam in chaos. The cabin becomes the warm womb, with dim lights and gently swinging hammocks, far far away from the frantic world above.

To return to events: at 2230 wind-driven rivulets of wind and water were skimming the waves, as happens at first, before their running fingers manage to grip the tops of the waves, turning them over like the hand holding the whip.

Watching the crew up on the yardarms shortening sail caused a little envy inside me. Looking upwards from under the mainmast, I could see that the main royal was yet to be stowed. At 2300 I found myself volunteering to climb. Three crewmembers in addition to myself, and an old man from another watch ascended, stopping to hold on, white-knuckled as a particularly large wave struck the ship. On the royal itself, the wind whistled past at 35 mph as with a beating heart I stepped onto the footrope.

I had made it. Now to do the job. My imagination was racing, headlines entering my head like arrows as I became conscious of only wearing a rope around my waist for safety.

The best part of working on a yard to furl a sail is the teamwork. Everybody works slowly and steadily with each other, driven by adrenaline and necessity. After a certain point, adrenaline stops pumping through the veins. It is replaced by pure life.

By the end of the evening, I had been aloft three times and the ship had been tacked, not an easy manoeuvre. I was tired, the sky vibrated when I blinked and I watched myself from two inches behind my own eyes. Pulling on ropes, slowly and steadily counting the hours ... the clock hands heaving round as if pulled by tiny, tired, sailors.

I awoke to find the wind died and most of the sails re-set. Jim had had a recurrence of his glandular fever and 14 hours of sleep seemed to do the trick. I was concerned when he was not on the watch and was subsequently relieved to find him asleep in his hammock, where he should be.

Throughout most of the night, the sun was up. The sky was clouded over but for dim shapes of light on the windward side. It was as if God was watching us and the remote flicker of the sun on the water extended a tiny thread to protect us all. God was to windward, watching from where we all should be.

14th

Swift evolution of events and sights limits my writing today. Suffice it to say that we have crossed the finish line and are heading up the beautiful Norwegian coast. 3 hours of stowing squaresails characterized the watch for me. At 10 o'clock we should arrive in some fjord, so no watches tonight but we cannot go ashore yet. Personally, I wish that we could have sailed for even longer.

1900 We are now proceeding up the fjord to arrive at perhaps 2200. The fjord stretches many miles into Norway, like a gulley cut into its very soul.

The scenery at the moment is truly spectacular. Clouds hang over the mountaintops, providing a ceiling and curtained veil for waterfalls to form trickling valleys into the basin. From the royal at sea I was the most powerful being alive, but now I am aware of being overpowered by the spire of the mountainous fjord.

Wordsworth wasted his time in Italy. The ancient cities held little for him. I think that he would have found a greater spiritual home in Norway, among the fjords, as Shelley did at Mont Blanc.

21

Preparing for the Pacific:
Autumn 2002

~·~

[Through the summer, Nicholas worked in a local second-hand bookshop and took his payment in books, reading doggedly towards his continuing ambition to get to Oxford and back into the company of Professor Wu and Michael Gearin-Tosh. In the autumn he got work as a waiter while he prepared for the next interview and for the Pacific voyage which seems, in retrospect, to be the pivot of his short life.]

Like so many others in countless generations past and present, I was a waiter. I grinned, sweated and apologized my way through four months in the Wentworth Hotel in Aldeburgh as part of my 'year out' from the educational rollercoaster which defines our young life.

I had finished A levels the previous summer and had achieved lower grades than expected: ABB. Despite having a place at St Andrew's University for September, a tugging urge inside of me forced me to turn it down and pursue a place at St Catherine's College Oxford. In a conversation with my mother, in which I, for some reason, found myself restraining tears, the decision had been made. I would take a gap year, fill in a UCAS form and once again, surf the bureaucratic wave.

I was on a family holiday in Canada when my results arrived and the final decision was taken. Had the leafy footpaths of Vancouver not been present to act as my mute counsellor over those few days, detaching me pleasantly from the torrent of reality, I may have received the news with much less dignity (not that there was anything particularly dignified about the way in which I did receive the news).

The prospect of having a year to fill was exciting. Every September for the past 13 years, my mother had been delivering me into the care of an educational institution, but this year was veiled in mystery. My imagination galloped around the possible, the impossible and the absurd as to what I might do with my time. Although people may never be truly free of obligation, a gap year can be the closest that you will ever come to this blissful state. Of course, I had university applications to go through and therefore studies to complete, but I did not mind so much since I had chosen for it to be this way.

It wasn't long before the first part of my year fell into place. One summer previously I had sailed from Nova Scotia to Holland on a Dutch square-rigger, *Europa*, and the captain now agreed to take me on as an apprentice deckhand for three months beginning in January. Until that time I was to study for my Oxford submission essays and interview; that is, if I got an interview. It was in this time that I also had to get a job of some sort. A part-time job, I hoped, would allow me to focus on studying without becoming lethargic. I would also save up enough money to help fund my sailing expenses.

A friend put me in touch with the Wentworth Hotel, a local family-run business. As luck would have it they took me on, to my immense gratitude, for I was completely inexperienced in any trade whatsoever. It seems to be a legal requirement, or at least a rite of passage, that everyone must spend a small portion of their youth as a waiter. Although unwilling to uphold any traditions of this kind, I somehow found myself darting between tables with an order pad for three months, shortly after finishing school. Although far from being the slickest waiter, preferring to resort to an amiable clumsiness to endear myself to customers, I quickly slipped into the routine .

First days in any new job must be taxing, and especially so with being a waiter. In an office there is relatively little harm in looking bemused and vague when you are new. As a waiter, however, I was instructed to appear confident and collected when amongst the guests. I therefore strode in and out of kitchen doors, broom cupboards and bedrooms, always trying to look businesslike and knowledgeable.

One thing that startled me on my first day was how much many of the guests resembled their food. The similarity became striking. An old, stout poached pear was calling me to bring coffee. Two half-lobsters, dressed in pink, required their main course while a rare Angus steak boomed to his bored colleagues, flushing in his red wine sauce.

It was strange that until I had worked in the hotel for about a month I never really looked at my surroundings. I suppose that I was too preoccupied with simply keeping up, so that I never noticed what a beautiful place it was. I remember clearly one breakfast time, on a Sunday. It had been dark when I arrived at 0630. As I was waiting for the first guests just after sunrise, rays of sunlight fell through the large glass windows, sparkling in the glasses and throwing patterns of light onto the carpet. The whole restaurant seemed to glow against the blue line of the barely visible sea. The tapestries on the walls looked as if a little life had been breathed into them; they became much more than a collection of stitches. They had energy, vibrancy and a loveliness which took my breath away.

The sun rose a little higher, scattering light around the room. Had I fallen asleep, or was time moving slightly differently for me than for everybody else? The coffee inside of me gave me a warm feeling, subduing active thoughts for a few magic minutes. For some reason this one, outwardly insignificant, morning is the dominating memory of my time as a waiter. I suppose that it was the first time that I had really taken to looking at my surroundings, to appreciate the beautiful substance which is formed when the mind and the physical coincide. Stephen Spender wrote:

What is precious is never to forget
The essential delight of the blood drawn from ageless springs
Breaking through rocks in worlds before our earth ...
Never to allow gradually the traffic to smother
With noise and fog, the flowering of the spirit.

When I worry that nothing in my mind is of significant value, or that what I write sounds cheesy or false, I think of this passage and of the importance of honesty even at the cost of the cynical contempt of others.

[In the midst this interlude at the hotel, the second Oxford interview happened. It was over a year before he wrote this detailed account of those days, but it follows here for the sake of chronology:]

I do not know exactly what force prompts me to make an account of my second interview experience. Perhaps it is more than simply a hedonistic recognition of my own achievement. Having been turned down by St Catherine's college the previous year, in the nicest possible way I might add, I felt somewhat less than fresh-faced on my subsequent return for the ill-advised second attempt. I could still remember the faces of the tutors and the corners of the rooms I would, once again, be awkwardly staring at. All in all, I felt as one might feel on returning to the site of a traumatic incident.

I signed in at the porter's lodge and was told to make my way to the JCR to check notice boards for interview times. On entering, the thought surfaced that the room I was about to walk into would contain people of unimaginable intelligence. Some, I was sure, would be like me but I still had a distinct sense of lowering the average IQ of the room. I even imagined the walls sucking in slightly as I entered.

A year before, when entering the common room for the first time,

I remember being confronted by the large television, the pool tables and amiable background noise. This year, however, memories of paranoid glances at the notice boards and nervous hours spent trying to skim-read the entire English canon before an interview flooded my head. The outside drizzle had made my shoulders damp, and physical discomfort built from social discomfort, forcing my retreat to my room.

Armed with the knowledge that nothing was going to happen to me until ten o'clock the next day, I set about re-reading my Personal Statement, to keep the details in my head:

'I was offered a university place to study English this year, but decided instead to take a gap year to read widely without the responsibilities of school. Over the past year my love of literature has grown immensely and I want to get the most from my degree course.

I have grown particularly fond of poetry, especially the romantics Keats, Coleridge and Shelley. T.S. Eliot and W.H. Auden are also particular favourites, and I am enjoying classic novels, from *Heart of Darkness* to *David Copperfield*. Theatre helps to open my eyes to possible interpretations of a text, some more innovative than others: I particularly liked Vanbrugh's *The Relapse*, the new *A Winter's Tale* and *The Crucible*.

At school I enjoyed Chaucer, Shakespeare and Milton. English S-level gave me a taste of Donne, Swift and others. For coursework I chose to examine visions of utopias from Plato to Thomas More to Aldous Huxley. In History I researched profit in the transatlantic slave trade, which was most enlightening. Physics A level gave me a certain mental agility. I am organized in my work, which enabled me to cope with illness in the first year of my A levels.

I was a school prefect, though not always a willing part of the system. Being head of juniors, instructing RAF cadets and skippering small yachts were valuable, but I learnt more by sailing in three Tall Ships races; especially an Atlantic crossing on a Dutch barque with a multinational crew. Being at sea for a month under sail is a good way to escape the modern perspective and understand aspects of life, and literature, in earlier centuries. The ship has taken me on as crew next spring, meanwhile I am a waiter (which provides the odd Orwellian nightmare).

I really want to study literature, properly and intensively, with people who care about it as much as I do. Whether I am reading *Crime and Punishment* or spending hours on a fragment of Yeats, I adore every minute. I believe that a private love of reading is the core of it, but know that I need tuition and discussion. I want the best that I can get. I know that turning down a firm offer and taking this reading year is a risk, but will not measure out my life in coffee spoons. My belief that I am suitable to do a classic English literature degree stems from involvement in the subject and what it reveals. I am confident that it is what I need to do.'

A prickly discomfort began to make itself apparent as I read my own pontifications about my partial knowledge. When writing the wretched thing, I had been completely comfortable in asserting my knowledge of Yeats, my profound understanding of Chaucer and unique empathy with the poetry of Donne. I berated myself for talking bullshit and prepared myself as best I could by trying to recollect what I had recently read of the plethora of poets mentioned in my statement. To complete my solitary evening, I delved into Tennyson's 'The Princess'. From this I felt inspired to don a blonde wig and female attire. The story of a Prince infiltrating an all-female college (by his own admission he looks like a girl) sparked off an intricate and paranoid dream about finding my way to the wrong college and finding the princess already drowned.

I was pleased to be woken up at 7.00 and have time to separate dream from reality. Sensible of needing a good breakfast and a good long stare at the notice boards, I made my way down to the dining hall. I was an hour early, in fact, but this was not a problem since several of my fellow interviewees were also shifting nervously from foot to foot, unsure of what to do or say. An inflated sense of significance pervaded the halls and common rooms throughout, as if our thoughts and deeds on this occasion were displayed on our countenances for all to see. Reading another person's thoughts is never easier than when you are in anticipation of the same event.

Although the first meeting was merely a friendly introduction, the tension among the English applicants seemed insoluble.

O! God. This is it. Oh my God. '*O lente, lente currite, noctes equi!*' raced through my mind and around the hallway. The event itself was not to be dreaded, after all: it was a simple introduction. The dread was in the forward motion of time, drifting me on unstoppably towards my fate.

The advice given to me in the first meeting proved to be more valuable than it first appeared. We were told not to be nervous and not to second-guess their actions. Most would suppose that this was the standard pacifying speech, designed to calm only the gullible. Not so. Second-guessing the motions and actions of the Catz tutors was later to get me needlessly almost to the point of illness. Of course, natural curiosity is permissible, but I would recommend a passive stance to anybody taking Oxford interviews. Your intellectual curiosity would be more wisely spent in a more creative way.

I digress. My first interview was for midday, which to my mind is a good time to have an interview. Everybody is awake by this stage, but not in a pre-lunch bad mood. I was informed that we would be questioned on our submission essays. Last year's experience had led me to expect a group interview of poetical discussion. I made haste towards my room to re-read my essays and make up excuses for them.

I emerged from my first interview satisfied with the way that it had gone. My interviewers had seemed interested in my essays and the discussion reminded me of why I was applying to Oxford in the first place. I wanted to study English with people who were as enthused about it as I was. I wanted tutors whose enthusiasm would further kindle my own. My first attempt to get a place at St Catz had given me a glimpse of the passion and enjoyment which goes hand-in-hand with literature. I did not regret my re-application, even if it all came to nothing. I had enjoyed the first interview and felt more relaxed for the rest.

At the end of the interview I was handed a poem and asked to verify whether or not I had seen it before. The purpose of this was to ensure that the piece was truly unseen. The thought behind the unseen close textual analysis is that the candidate's reaction to the poem is honest and basic, untempered by excessive or inadequate schooling. This method allows candidates from different educational backgrounds to compete on an even basis. Or so I now believe, since I cannot say for sure.

My poem was 'Love III' by George Herbert. I believe that for the rest of my life, when I read this poem I will feel a shudder.

Love bade me welcome, yet my soul drew back,
        Guilty of dust and sin.
But quick-ey'd Love, observing me grow slack
        From my first entrance in,
Drew nearer to me, sweetly questioning
        If I lack'd anything.

'A guest,' I answer'd, 'worthy to be here';
        Love said, 'You shall be he.'
'I, the unkind, the ungrateful? ah my dear,
        I cannot look on thee.'
Love took my hand and smiling did reply,
        'Who made the eyes but I?'

'Truth, Lord, but I have marr'd them; let my shame
        Go where it doth deserve.'
'And know you not,' says Love, 'who bore the blame?'
        'My dear, then I will serve.'

'You must sit down,' says Love, 'and taste my meat.'
So I did sit and eat.

All my good spirits from the previous interview were shattered at precisely 1440. Having entered the room (the walls of which were still hung with anxiety from the previous year) and exchanged unconscious niceties I was asked if I would like to read out the poem. The interview might have gone better if I had simply said 'NO!'. A verbal stumble through the grammatical corridors of George Herbert did nothing to calm my spirits. I was then asked, in a peremptory way, if I would like to tell them about the poem. I went though it line by line, after which ensued an awkward silence. I had been wrong. In a nervous pre-interview frenzy, I had overlooked one of the key aspects of the poem. What the hell was 'Love's meat'? Like a lamb to the slaughter I was led to the answer. I felt like getting up and leaving the room in tears. I had actually blown it. So much mental preparation and anticipation had been poured into these 20 minutes, and here I was floundering about like an idiot; failing to think, having all confidence drained out of me.

The worst thing about it all was that, true to their word, they were not asking trick questions. I was floundering because of myself, not because I was being misled by confounding tactics or subtle Socratic ironies. This thought was the twist of the knife for me. It was my fault.

I was asked, as with all candidates, to step outside the interview room briefly while they decided what to do with me. I felt truly sorry for any flies which may have been on the wall of that room at the time. I looked, in a detached way, at the interviewee who was to follow me. She, like me, was studying a sheet of paper as if to take her eyes off it would surely mean her doom. I thought to myself 'would it not be superbly ironic if she were studying some familiar favourite of mine?' Would it not crown the whole experience if I went away thinking that I could have been given that poem? Curiosity forced me to glimpse at the sheet of paper and, sure enough, 'Sailing to Byzantium' stared back at me. Oh why, oh why. What a delicious yet tragic irony. In the few seconds I had, I wished her good luck and re-entered the room to hear my fate. I was free to go for the rest of the day, but might be required tomorrow.

At this point I was certain that I had failed. The college grounds seemed to assume a dull, penetrating silence, the kind of silence one hears after the last gunshot echo has died away. I made my way back to my room and cried tears of self-indulgent frustration. I thought about all the people who had helped me and supported me. I could not even say that I had given it my best shot. Nervousness had prevented me from being my best, and my fuck-up had been indefensibly blatant.

I remember gazing down at Auden's 'Musee des Beaux-Arts' and wondering if, just as in my interview, I had been missing the point of all poetry. Was there a deeper shade of meaning to poetry which I had always skimmed over? For the first time in four years I considered the possibility that I was just not suitable for an English degree. I had thought hard about 'Love III' and had failed to extract a proper meaning. Perhaps I often satisfied myself with explanation rather than meaning. I thought that my throat would rip open at this point. The so-often idealized world of happy fantasy was tearing against an uncertain reality, each forming an irresistible retreat. The connection between my actions and their consequences seemed to be in that very room, like a demon who must be faced.

Of course, I somewhat overreacted, but I am told that the first registered expression of a man being stabbed is surprise, and my reaction was equally irrational. It was not that any of the tutors were at all rude, quite the opposite, but at the time I truly believed that the approaching night would be my last in St Catherine's.

It pains me to admit it, a strapping 19 year old lad as I am, but all I wanted to do was phone my mother. She was in Oxford at the time and I needed a face-to-face talk with somebody. The sooner I could discuss my experience, the sooner I could gain a little perspective on the situation. Normally, I would have read a little and felt a lot better, but the very sight of a poem seemed to fill me with a sense of revulsion for the time being. A sour cappuccino in Starbucks and a chat did not make me feel any better as such, but gave me an anchor in reality which was much needed. After pacing, muttering and the odd disgusted glance at a poetry book I went to bed at 8.30 in a sea of self-pity. Speculation overwhelmed me. I could stand the despair, it was the hope that troubled me.

I awoke, after a dreamless sleep, dispirited but back to earth and prepared to consider the university alternatives.

[In fact, Nick's third interview went well; he spoke with passion for fifteen minutes 'to show them at least that I'm not an idiot' and the tutors decided to take him. After a couple of terms they were to feel so well vindicated that he was given an exhibition scholarship in recognition of his work. However, characteristically, the retrospective account of his interview process breaks off just as his success was about to happen. It merely continues thus, and startlingly:]

I am now tired of writing this piece. I felt the same at the time. I wanted to scrap the chapter which I had just written and re-start.

But certain actions cannot be undone. Therefore I shall keep this piece, as a monument to the honesty which brought no man fame or fortune.

What is important is to remember that it is not the way in which we record our existence, but that we do record it. In the air, and everywhere around, we must remember how the streets ring out for every soul that thought and felt and passed through them in weakness and in strength.

We will be joined together with our soul if we can feel the glorious delight in every life, inscribed around us, which waits for us to come and truly see the inspiration every being brings, recorded in our lifes' empathy. I truly believe that we cannot erase our deeds, but move to justify our doings.

> [Back now to the hotel narrative, just as Nicholas himself returned to work while he waited for the verdict from Oxford. The Pacific voyage was growing closer ...]

I would like to relate another instance which particularly affected me during this time. A birthday function, held in the hotel one evening. There were about 16 people around a long table at the far end of the restaurant as I recall. As the birthday cake emerged, the woman whose 40th it was said 'I'm either going to cut the cake or my throat'. 'Suit yourself' was the only response offered from one of the waitresses. Needless to say, the cake was cut. But why was it said, especially to a strange waitress? Why sulk when 15 people surround you, present because of you? At the time I was mystified.

For the first time, I began to see how 10 years could be swallowed up in an occupation such as this without being noticed. The comfort and domestic familiarity of the particular hotel had a mysterious ability to ensnare the staff as well as customers, and as a smoker wakes up one morning with cracked lips and a bloodstained pillow, a revulsion grew inside me for what I had become. After such a short period of time I had become torpid and lost all desire to travel. I had known all along that my employment would be short, and of the adventure to come, but what lay ahead looked to me like fragments of glass distorted in a kaleidoscope. Discussions with friends and hotel guests about my journey were distant and vague. I knew that I would board the ship in Costa Rica, which often got switched to Puerto Rico in an absent conversational manner. I knew that I would end up in Japan. But as to the route, it never entered my consciousness. I did not care.

In short, I had become too comfortable. I became attached to the Wentworth. I had started to look around with greater care, and the intrinsic warmth of the place became apparent. This aside, I was pleased to take my leave of it on Christmas Day. I fumbled my way through a last breakfast shift and said goodbye to my co-workers.

I enjoyed working on Christmas Day for two reasons. Firstly, the excitement of moving on, combined with the childish (and I should point out that childish could never be a pejorative term for me) excitement of it being Christmas Day. Secondly, with a giant hotel Christmas lunch impending, I wanted to see the type of person who also ate a cooked breakfast.

So on Christmas Day I sweated and apologized my way through my last shift and said goodbye to my work colleagues, some of whom had worked in the hotel for over 20 years and will probably continue to do so for many more.

The Pacific Crossing

The nature and route of my journey, with which I soon familiarized myself, was this. I was to sail on a Dutch square-rigger named *Europa*, from the Pacific coast of Costa Rica to Nagasaki, Japan, stopping en route in Hawaii, Johnston Island, Pohnpei in Micronesia, Saipan and finally Nagasaki. I had made a previous trip on board, across the Atlantic as a paying trainee. I was returning as a volunteer crewmember, or apprentice. Even before I had given the voyage much real thought I knew that there would be a big difference between now being effectively an employee, and my previous time as a guest trainee. More would be expected of me, and from the lounge of the Wentworth Hotel I did not believe I could deliver.

Christmas and New-year fled past in their cosy domestic way. Dark corners of rooms shone with tinsel, while firelight danced along it. I felt wrapped in a blanket of homeliness through this time, as if what was past, passing and to come was an irrelevancy. I remember that on New Year my family went off to my uncle's house to celebrate the arbitrary moment. Having decided to remain behind, my inebriated attention wandered on to the situation now and a year ago. Last year I had no university place, no upcoming adventure and a heap of A-level work to complete. This year I had my place at the university of my dreams, and a huge adventure to come. As to work, all the work which lay ahead was only of my choosing. I would work on a ship and study English literature. For the first of many times in the following months I believed life has an amazing way of picking up, and that work is not, and never will be, just work.

Work at school had been crushing, deadening at times. But work can also stimulate and uplift the senses once you are in a position to make the choices for yourself. I only write this ramble because if it is ever read by somebody in their A level year, it is important that they are told that there is something better waiting. Anybody who tells you that youth is the best time of your life has, quite frankly, misunderstood life. All through history we can see the best times of man have been in the transitory phases. Transition has always nurtured optimism. The early days of the Communist era, the opening up of the American West, the founding of American independence. And so it is with every life. A level times are the times of least change and therefore the least optimism. Metaphorically, you are in Stalin's Russia, the revolutionary greatness having faded. Only when you emerge from school does the tide of change in your life renew your optimism, your joie-de-vivre to use the old cliché. A levels have no business in the world of sensitive individuals and absolutely no business to call themselves work. They are drudgery. They do not test or resemble knowledge, they simply test the limits of how far you will go down the path of moral destruction for relatively little reward. Hang in there. Browning began an inspirational journey on the morn of Rome and May, and so shall you.

Although I had a sense of how great what was approaching was to be, a nervous uneasiness grew inside me as the time for departure approached. My packing was done over the course of several days, and too often I would sit down and lose myself in a book, or guzzle Christmas chocolate, instead of concentrating on what I actually needed. A strange rope seemed to be binding me to my home, and I even dreamt in this period that I went away from home and returned to find my family dead and burnt.

I add in parenthesis that dreams, both waking and unconscious, form such a large portion of my life that reference to them is sometimes unavoidable. Sometimes I have lain awake trying to exorcise them. But these accounts are for the future. I rely on the reader's good taste to compensate for my authorial inadequacies and remove from memory all overly familiar prose which lack of self-control compels me to scribble.

In many cheerful moments, packing was fun. As I laid up various outdoor gadgets, knives, torches and so on, my imagination wandered over the times that I might need them. I imagined daring situations aloft where a pocket-knife could be invaluable, and filled my packing time in such a way. As with many episodes in my life I allowed a hazy, often feeble fantasy to take the place of reality, which was watching me like a vulture ...

The truth is, I was afraid. I was afraid to change my surroundings or change myself. How might I return from my travels? Would I hate the books which had served as my friends? Would I despise my university and make decisions I could not conceive to be monstrous mistakes at the time? O heaven help the mind that's flexible!

34

On Arriving In Costa Rica, January 2002

Let's have one drink, to prove we're really here
(I cast my eyes into the gloomy bar)
We raised a glass to prove that we were there,
Across an ocean leaning on a bar
With midnight moisture dancing on the air
And hazy thrills which play around the heart.
It is in these small moments that I fear
The world: insanities I don't record
But which drive dreams along their wild career
Striking imagination's sombre chords
Entering through the key which locks my room
And shaping terror out of everything
That comes into our minds from their vast gloom.

Let's have one drink, to prove we're really here,
In half an hour, in that dim lit bar …
The words of my companion spelt out fear
Deciphered in my young and weary heart.
Why should I fear? the world today is swell,
I've conquered ocean in six hours flat
Yet … miserlike – I cannot cross the hall
I cannot bear to turn, expose my back
For the short second while I lock my room
And 'click' just like the loading of a gun.
I cried into the Costa-Rican gloom
And small faint voices offering me some fun.
A question in my head enters the room
And chances 'Honey, are you here all alone?'

[Email home, same night]

Dear Mum,

Thanks for your words of encouragement. We have just spoken on the phone. With any luck I will be able to get the correct visa but if not, I am sure that everything will work out OK.

I hope that everything at home is all right. Give my regards to Rose, Dad and the rest of the family.

I am quite looking forward to the first month and a half but I have my doubts about going all the way to Nagasaki. I am afraid that the whole crossing may be a bit much for me (whatever this makes me, so be it). I will give it a fair try, however until Hawaii.

All my love, Nick

[The voyage to Hawaii, despite all misgivings, was a good one: short-handed, only 17 people aboard. There is no detailed log but from Hawaii came these emails:]

Hi Dad

I have arrived in Hawaii and have had a great time on passage. I Have found out that I have the wrong type of visa and the authorities say that I cannot leave the ship. Oh well ... They cant have their own way all the time. I should be OK so long as I stay out of trouble. The only drawback is that I can't use my passport to cash travellers cheques (It is safer locked up in the ship where they can't see it.) Because of this, I cannot afford to use the computer for very long.

Down to business. I cannot get any phones to work so I hope you get this email soon. I hope that everybody at home is good. It is heartwarming to receive so many emails from friends and if I can get hold of some money, I will send emails to them all. If not, give them my sincerest apologies (I will try my utmost to get some money).

Anyway, I am having a great time and will be back in contact somehow.

Nick

[And to his schoolmates, this:]

From: Nick Heiney <alastor1815@hotmail.com>
Subject: Aloha from nick.

Hello RHS.
I hope that you are all well and not working too hard!
30 days after setting off from Costa Rica, the *Europa* has finally arrived in Hawaii and everybody is taking a well earned break. It already feels strange to say goodbye to some of the crew as they go to resume their lives in the real world. We had only 15 people on board for the crossing as opposed to 45 when I crossed the Atlantic. When a ship is short handed, everybody works very hard and also grows very close. It is a fantastic learning experience to have to be able to take in sail all by yourself and operate a vast amount of the ship's equipment independently. I have already learnt a lot and have become conscious of how much I still have to learn.

The passage itself went really well. It seems like only yesterday that we sailed off the anchor in Puntareanas, a month ago. The rotating 2 watch system on board makes the days flow seamlessly into one another and nobody can quite believe that an entire month has gone by without sight of land.

Unusually for the stretch of ocean we were in, the trade winds never kicked in for more than about 48 hours at a time and we had variable wind strengths and directions throughout the passage. This gave us an opportunity to experiment constantly with studding sails and strange, rotting pieces of canvas which the Boatswain would drag up from the bowels of the ship and insist that we set. Inevitably, this enthusiasm lead to a lot of sail sewing as God began to remove the more delicate sails for us.

Life on board ship as a non-paying crewmember has shown me a very different aspect of sailing to that of the paying trainee. As a crewmember, you work on a 2 rather than 3 watch system. Sleep and sleep management become all the more important in these watches since it is difficult to catch up on sleep in 3 or 4 hour snatches. Also, during one spell 3 days out from Honolulu, the wind went from a force 1 to a high force 7 in the space of 15 minutes. I was up in the bosun's chair scrubbing backstays at the time and it was spectacular to watch the black clouds roll over the sky and the sea going from flat calm to 4.5 meter swells so quickly. The direction of the gale and the suddeness with which it caught us meant that the yardarms were aback and we had to kick our way out onto the yardarms against a lot of flogging canvas. Being short handed, everybody had to work hard to bring in the sails before we could brace round. The watches worked hard that night, going aloft almost every half hour to bring in or loose out sails. The rough weather pulled us together and showed us the importance of knowing our knots and lines as we fumbled around in the swells looking for the right lines.

Our arrival in Hawaii was made difficult by the coastguard who ordered us to leave US waters for 24 hours while they completed paperwork. When we had finally docked, I was told by the immigration authorities that I had the wrong type of visa and could not set foot ashore. By avoiding trouble and anybody in a coastgaurd uniform, I seem to be OK ashore at the moment.

Anyway, I am having the time of my life here and hope to continue to do so for at least another 2 months. I hope that everybody is well and happy. I would thoroughly recommend sailing a tall ship as crew to anybody who enjoys adventure.

Kindest regards,
Nick Heiney

Pacific Logs,
February–June 2002

[This introduction, written a year or so later, was part of a resolution to write up the whole voyage formally. It lays out his beliefs in why such things are written, but got no further: when it ends, we return to the daily log written on board.]

Travel writing in the past has often been inspiring and informative. These days we can look at a Lonely Planet guide, a traveller's published diary, a television programme or a literary work to learn something about a foreign land. If we chance to look at one of the more profound travel accounts it is possible to gain a level of empathy with the traveller and imaginatively connect with a country and age. As a first-time writer I am left asking the question, 'How do I get my experience across?'.

I want to convince people that what I went through and saw was something which is worth sharing, but not lay myself bare or reveal myself as an egotist. This immediately precludes much of my diary, which I kept religiously (by that I mean occasionally, and out of guilt). The diary only reflects what I was able to write at the time. There are many – Anne Frank being the obvious example, Robin Knox Johnston being the better example – whose thoughts are metered, and whose diaries are subsequently of value to a reader. My diary is full of adolescent angst, not worthy of publication in itself but of some value when I try to remember my feelings.

What remains for my style of narration? Hundreds of options, I suppose, but one of the most appealing has to be the persona. I could be like Plath or Kerouac, talking from behind a mask. People would know it was me, so I would get the credit, but I could weave fictions, centralise or remove myself at will.

This option gives me the most power over what I write, hence I must dismiss it. Events that occured did actually occur. I just don't feel that I have the licence to use authorial power to distort a narration into allegory, which it ultimately would be. It would be the review of the critical book, or an account of some small event. I have facts as a skeleton, feelings as organs and reserve for skin. My work does not need a mask, it only needs a reader to give it eyes.

At this point, I feel bad. If I cannot write from a persona because I would have too much power then I definitely cannot be an omniscient narrator, looking down on facts, looking at myself. I shall make a rule. I am allowed to be ecstatic, in other words to step outside of myself to get a better view. However *I will never look at myself when I am doing this.*

Maybe I should write a technical manual. I could talk about how a ship works, how to tack, how to clean, how to bake a loaf of bread or calculate due west from the sun's azimuth. A problem arises here too. What do I have to say about such things which has not already been copiously written about? How could I contribute to the literature of the subject? I couldn't; and also, what would be the point? More informed sources than myself have greater eloquence and understanding of these subjects. I was a deckhand, and not an experienced one. Technicalities were never my speciality. Speciality is not my speciality.

My choice now seems obvious, I should simply start from the beginning, use my diaries as an aide-memoire and relate from start to finish what I went through, letting chronology dictate my structure. The only problem with this approach to my experience is that it limits the range of observations that can be made. For instance, 'the wind played lyrical notes in the rigging' is an absurd thing to say if I am taking the reader into the present tense. I would not be saying the right thing, and yet there is much less satisfaction in saying 'the wind made a high pitched noise in the rigging' which is what it actually did. The ship is made of cold iron, not flesh.

To be true to myself this account must be derived from both memory and sensation (what is one without the other?). So how does the memory work? What is clearest in my mind? Of course, it is the time when I left the ship for good. What is my least clear memory? It is boarding the ship in a heat-haze for the first time, and the few weeks after that. It appears that my memory works backwards. If I believed that the sky was exploding, it is not because it was, but because it was in my imaginative memory and, as I have just discovered, my memory works backwards. Therefore, if I begin my account in Costa Rica, I have circumvented the process of reaching back into memory and past sensations. Rather than sliding backwards, I would have jumped indelicately backwards and upset the remembering process. If I can truthfully write what I thought and felt, as far as truth applies to such abstracts, I must write my account starting from the most recent events. I shall reach back from them, trying to untangle my web of activity.

Most travel accounts unknowingly have fallen into the trap of working against memory.

I shall work with memory, because I want to raise ghosts, to watch ocean skies burn again, and feed my spirit into old imaginings. I shall not alter time for the sake of memory because the two are one and the same.

Hawaii and Beyond: The Onboard Log

'I wish for that which idle wish will gain
For zealous action dulls ambition's flame
And the dewdrop has no beauty in a storm
But calm blue skies will lend it grace again'
                                        (A.G. Fox)

So I have now been on *Europa* since January 9th. Just over 40 days. Thoughts of home are slowly vanishing and I am able to enjoy the experience. The escape from domesticity is always an aid to self-discovery. I have come to realize that my home is a lonely place, dislocated from friendship and the strong emotions which now flood my heart. From sunset to sunrise a sustaining energy seems to run through the ship. People are always awake, always working. The emotional roller-coaster (I forgive myself the vulgarity) works to make me feel alive. Alive, as if the word which was a biological fact before has become a spiritual certainty.

'These are thy wonders, Lord of love ...
Bringing down to hell and up to heaven in an hour' (George Herbert)

As each day passes, I become sensible of a stronger emotion: an emotion forged by a small group on an inexplicably large ocean. It crushes and redeems in a way I never knew was possible.

Right now the ocean swells which have kept our small ship company since Costa Rica are rolling us onward towards Pohnpei. In a way it is a shame that we cannot to go Johnston Island and that the Saipan cruise has been cancelled, but it cannot be helped in the modern world of professional sailing. I am just grateful to be on the simple end of proceedings. In offices in Holland or in the Captain's quarters, issues of what man has made of man must be constantly quarrelled over and reconciled.

'I will not travel west only to reach the easternmost coast' is the way I like to think at the moment. However long or short, an experience is complete. Whatever can be deduced from it is a secondary consideration. What we learn is less important than the shadow learning casts, which becomes absorbed into our very souls.

In a stolen moment I found myself gazing at the silver trail of the moon. It danced upon the ocean's infinite and mysterious depths. I began to wonder if it was a silver shaft of heaven that I saw, diluted in the waters of the world so that mortal man could gaze upon a fragment of the divine majesty. ...

40

I then turned to the dazzling moon itself,
That I might see a clearer view
Of something perfect and austere.
What was it but a shiny silver orb to me
When I first cast my eyes upon the heaven-pacing form?
Could an orb of barren mountain be a subject of such strong
    poetry?
But then I gazed and kept a conference
With what to me seemed an inanimate object
Of limited and hazy, weak romance.
Through sleepy eyes I watched its sullen gaze,
Until there came a moment of release -
And every crater glowed infinitely brighter.

It was as if the moon was giving up the secrets which it had held for
all time. The corona shone so brightly that there appeared an eye
which gazed into recesses of my soul. Beyond ideals and the
restrictions of metaphysics, knowledge of the all-consuming truths
frightened me, and I wept.

That night I slept under the stars and woke to see great cloud
mountains on the horizon. Silver and devastating. I wondered if I was
still dreaming. My mind played in those mountains for some time.
The silvery pyres above bred weak-minded fantasy, in which I existed
for a time in perfect balance with the world around.

I find that one of the best things about working with a professional
crew is that there is no feeling that people must shout or scream to
make their orders clear. People simply fulfil their tasks in the simplest
and most efficient way possible.

O let the hour of fantasy dissolve
To show the clearer light of poetry!
And let the crystal shapes of life resolve
Into a creature, fantastic and free
To conquer shadow in an age of gold,
Where time itself will know no passing glee.
Although our stagnant earth may still revolve
We shall rejoice in divine clarity
For God himself in splendour shall descend
On wings of sunrise with his angel train
And linger in our hearts for one moment
That we may work towards him once again.
    O gallop on, wild horses of the night!
    For even you may glimpse eternal light.

It is strange how a word can shape your day, if not your life. The right phrase from the right person can echo in your mind and in your dreams like a floating ghost. For hours now I have been wondering about a line. The merest hint given by a friend, of immeasurable pain in her life. It emerged in casual conversation, as a tangle emerges in an un-knotted rope.

When somebody that I care about creates a dark shadow as a part of their impression, it is sheer agony. O, if death could visit me, torment me for eternity if just to take away this person's pain, dear God, let it fall upon me like Satan's rage! For nobody deserves less to be followed by a shadow, when they are created of such brilliant lightness. Let this be no idle wish if souls share any connection whatsoever. Retrace the soul's history to the time when we were one.

7th.

Overcast skies roll us onward to Pohnpei. On this leg, I have ceased to count the days at sea. Time has simply lurched by in four-hour watches, interrupted by terrible dreams, wrought from a troubled mind which it is difficult to admit possessing during the day.

The nature of one particular dream has been troubling me for a week now and makes me dread my rest-times.

> I dreamed that we were plagued by glassy Seas
> And that the ship was rotting from a sun-induced disease
> The timbers tore away my crewmates' flesh
> And gaping rusty holes were edged with blood.
> As days wore on, the crew began to feel resentment towards me,
> For they did think that I, alone unhurt
> Was the sole cause of all the torment which they had to face.
> So in the dead of night, whispers began
> To form deep shadows of conspiracy
> And whispers reached my ears where I lay
> In the blissful sleep of young first love
> Musing on the sweetest loveliness
> That man has ever felt in ages past.
>
> In all consuming omnipotence
> Which is peculiar to troubled dreams
> I felt their eyes burn into me like knives
> Ruining the beauty of the sea.
> In their diseased countenance their gazes
> Shot into my soul like fishooks
> And as resentful feelings swell up fast

The sea began to boil –
    And then, at last,
A hurricane began to take the ship
Along a path beyond all our control
Towards the centre of the seething mass.
The seas foamed and the water seemed insufficiently dense
    to support the ship;
But the crew were not afraid
Because the storm was born of their rage
And everybody knew where we were driven.

Insubstantial time wore on until an island hove into view. To us, it was as if a mountain's cap had risen out of the sea, bleak, barren and heartless. No sooner had I caught sight of the lightning-crowned mountain than I was flung onto its base with a mighty crack. At the same instant, the shining cloud and a lowering fog tugged the surface of the sea. Forces beyond the conscious or subconscious pushed the path of my dream up the dry, sandy mountain path, lifeless in any degree, until I had reached the summit.

A voice, as if woven from the very silence which it opposed, began; and as my mind began to slide from dimension to dimension, from will to powerlessness, I began to understand what it was saying.

The Approach to Pohnpei
[version apparently rewritten in tranquillity
a year later]

In the Pacific trade winds a sailor will often talk about the slipping by of time, how two days seem to turn into twenty without any conscious interval. The days are punctuated by blazing skies, feathery pink at sunrise and vividly fiery in the evening. The ship becomes like a metronome which has been attached to a human heart. Sometimes a breaking wave excites this heart: the helmsman's hands cannot correct the course and the ship sways more violently, straining alternately at the rigging to port and starboard. The crew conform to the rhythms of seconds, watches, days and passages with a huge sense of well-being. Many of my shipmates have vivid dreams of navigating the ship through city streets. My dreams have become too vivid. I dream of islands where the dead go to watch angels die. Lying on deck at night, watching the stars roll in and out from under the sails, I could not help feeling infinitely small, yet in such good company.

This is the third attempt I have made to write about this particular section of my voyage. the details are always present in my mind but they are difficult to resolve. In retrospect I would say that the twenty days which began with the approach to Pohnpei and ended in our arrival at Saipan were some of the best of the trip, the best of my life in fact.

The ripples which abandoned the shores of Costa Rica had been built up by the trade winds into magnificent ocean swells, some breaking on the rocky reefs of Hawaiian islands, some continuing with us, crested and bullish. Often in the gentle swaying of the ship offwatch dreams were interrupted, and the helmsman struggled, as one of the waves focused its energies on our hull with a small turret of dilating spray. Twenty-five days changed landmade tiredness to pleasant haziness, through which the beauty and lucidity of the sea became consuming.

The first indication that our voyage was ending was a mass of grey cloud in the sky. The forest zephyrs of Pohnpei sent up moisture, spreading out in a gigantic mass of cloud which in turn caused 300 days of rain per year, making the land fertile in its cycle. I had been up since four, carrying out routine maintenance, thoughtfully, with the spectre of land in my mind. As the sun rose it split the sky, a seam of gold through the cloud, making the island look somehow unreal. It barely distinguished itself from the mountains of silver trade wind clouds which had been the crux of my waking dreams since leaving Hawaii. Drowsily, we all looked at the shadow land, hot cups of coffee melting into our hands, anticipating ends and beginnings. The wind was the same as it ever was, the land had not yet disturbed the sea as we climbed aloft to stow the sails, shaking morning dew from the rigging as we grasped the nightcold wire stays. The sails billowed slightly in their gear as if they were eager to take the ship the last bit of the way into dock. For the first time in 3000 miles they were tied up, reduced to ornaments as the sound of engines began to fill the world.

When in dock we set to breakfast. Flies began to infest the deck, then the hatchways, then the galley as we raced them for the fresh fruit and bread rolls. This was a distant port, the least lonely nowhere in the world. This was a port through which all manner of ships passed on their journey between the superpowers. If you journey into the jungles as we did, there are ancient ruins among the swampy rivers, created by the old superpowers, who must have moved tonnes and tonnes of stone to build a jungle city. I asked a young child how it was believed that the stones got there. He gave an answer, more sensible than my question, that they 'flew there by magic'. Water has carved itself around the ancient city but left it untouched; beaten by sun and rain it was survived as if it were connected to the forest. Inside I saw the moss and roots among the stone, making the construction look as if it too had grown from the ground.

On the final night in port I was not company. Some of the crew who had become dearest to me were leaving and we were to change captains. I walked alone and heard the barking of dogs, subdued by day and enlivened in the tropical night. I felt inhuman, recessed into the same darkness which made the chained dogs growl and grind their fangs as I passed.

Often when we meet people, we have something in common with them. What I found on board *Europa* was that I had very little in common with any of my friends. Somehow, our experiences had led us to a common spiritual ground. Our ambitions had begun in different places and converged briefly at this point. It seems that free spirits make the best companions. When in their company, my background seemed more like a launch-pad than an aspect of self definition. Life was colourful and exciting, this was why I travelled, to be reborn from every dark mood and revel in my silliness.

[From Pohnpei, this email:]

Hi MUM.

I am afraid that, having crossed the dateline and gone through yet another timezone, it will be difficult to phone you. But never mind. The passage went well with pretty good winds all the way. The Saipan cruise has, as far as I know been cancelled. Therefore all dates have changed. I am definitely on until Nagasaki unless they throw me off the ship.

Most of the passage details you can get from the internet site but for myself, the passage went unbelievably quickly and I ceased to keep a record of the days. For me, the international dateline is the line after which all dates become meaningless.

I hope everything at home is alright (but if anything is not, you must must must tell me). Pohnpei is a pleasant place which has 300 days of rainfall per year. We went swimming in a waterfall and to see some ancient ruins, chewed betel nut and scrubbed rust off the hull.

Love
Nick

[This email to the school:]

> Hi RHS!
>
> Just a quick email to say that the Europa has arrived in Pohnpei and is due to be setting off again early tomorrow morning. We enjoyed fair winds on the passage from Honolulu (although the rolling was unbelievable at times). The highlight of the trip had to be catching a 60 kilo black marlin which took over an hour to get in and cost us a length of rope and a boathook. I will write more in 11 days time when I reach Saipan.
>
> Cheers
> Nick

Pohnpei to Saipan, via Nonwin Atoll: Onboard Log

Pohnpei-Saipan 16th day 2

Klaas joined the ship in Pohnpei. Goodbyes proved to be difficult and I was more tearful than most. At school I shook about five hands and that was it. Here I was hugged and talked to with sincerity. It was heartbreaking to wave goodbye to people who had come to mean so much to me.

Feelings of woe soon evaporated as we sailed out past the reef in a brisk 17 knots of wind, all working to set sails and fly. Pohnpei vanished into the light rainy mists like a half-retrieved memory, and we were once again out in the Pacific Ocean, new faces and old all co-operating, all bonded by the desire to set sail.

One more issue plagues my mind and that is that I am a fool. I have set myself up for a fall, from love and innocence, either by my speech or lack of it. When someone's mind cannot be read and you find yourself caring more about their emotions than your own, a conflict arises, fundamental to the purer side of human nature.

Ship

We two, like horses on the waves
Ran through the canyons blue.
And all that lonesome sailors crave
Was running round with you.

46

You were a Lucy, O my love
And I, a troubled soul
We saw cloud hills move on above,
And chose our course to roll.

We have watched the trade-wind swells begin to form off the shores of Costa Rica. Some break as surf on Hawaiian coasts, others glide on to Micronesia, gather might and engulf atolls, lapping upon the shores of Pohnpei. Some accompany us still as foam-topped couriers bound for lands beyond our reach.

The day our wave breaks upon the shores of Japan will be the consummation of delight and dread.

The Pacific Ocean is the least lonely place on earth. Birds land on deck, whales and dolphins have accompanied us and in such good company, loneliness seems a mere figment of the land. To look upon an empty sea and say that it is empty is not to look on it at all. As the squalls roll on past us, we feel truly like a part of the ocean.

17th 3rd day

I am low, in a dip so to speak. We have just caught a baby dorado and they decided to kill it. I painted the radar gantry in the swells, which proved to be difficult. I feel lonely in the new crew. I do not really sit with them anymore and I feel as if my friends are being pulled away. In my experience, this feeling will pass . The biggest challenge is not letting my dip affect others. By being glad to be in their company, I am achieving this. Every time a surge of bad emotions comes, I think of angels and try to wash the feeling away. Not suppress it, but purge it completely.

18th 4th day

We are at Nonwin Island. The water is flat and a pleasant breeze is flowing over the ship, making sleep a positive joy. I had a good talk at sunrise which left me sad, but showed me the route to reality, much needed. The atoll emerged from the mist … for now, I am tired.

Having been ashore, I hold a place in my heart for such an island. The warmth of human spirit everywhere sometimes overwhelms me. Every object makes a voyage, every person is infinitely complex if only one could see. The spirit which continues our race, the spirit which founded Rome and realized how unimportant it is, was in the air and every hopeful eye I see.

Perhaps too much beauty has the power to crush us. When what is in our minds cannot compare to what we receive from the world around: the islands, the artwork, the Spirit will outlive us. Shining and beautiful for what to us is an eternity.

If I could spread the wings of my spirit and become a sunrise and hang over all the earth where there is no heart to swell with love but only beauty to absorb it, I would be content. What I have seen today and every day is a monument to the eternity in which we all partake. To see the person I care about most in the world acknowledge this beauty in such an excess of joy relieves the pain, and makes my lack of simple truth a figment of the complex beauty which has run through the earth since the first spirit brushed the first creature on an empty planet.

These words are sickness. They deride the human form and attempt to replace it with the aetherial. The history of the soul yields no history. The history of man yields only mystery. Events present no reconciliation and we should hope for none.

Now may sleep make me a better man, and may I always remember the shining moments of beauty in the eyes of others. I think of those who are great until I need no longer look to an individual presence. No skin-touched soul shines as bright as the soul from uncreated boundaries. Now at peace, may I die.

19th

Yesterday was again spent at the atoll. I had a dip in the morning, largely due to exhaustion – sleep and waking have become dreaded to me and in my fatigue I painted the mizzen top and moused it, returning to deck when my arms burnt inwardly and outwardly.

I went ashore in a foul mood, hoping only to stretch my legs. The afternoon was more wonderful than I ever could have hoped. I played with the children all afternoon and ate coconut. Myself, Ric, Erica and John played volleyball against the islanders. On returning to the ship on a high, I dipped after a certain conversation, memorable only to myself. I prayed upon the rising crescent moon that I would not survive another night. That love could crush my subtle form and waves of emotion could wash my soul into eternity.

I woke in tears and vowed (in foolishness) to waste my days in corridors of dreams. I fed upon the deadliest of loves.

This morning we set sail. I was slow, embarrassed and did not care.

22nd

Yesterday was a bad day. My throat burned, sapping the energy from me. I must learn to control my lows and handle my highs, although they have been few and far between recently.

Could anybody ever love me? Can I be redeemed from loneliness? Sometimes I feel that I will never know.

Nonwin Island gave me a glimpse of redemption. The flatness of the atoll giving it a beautiful vulnerability, almost as fragile as the way of life it supports. One man told me that the world was ending. I also found out from him that he had never been further than Yap. I suppose perhaps that if your world is infinitely small, the ending is easier to contemplate. When a storm could destroy the fragile balance, the end is an easier concept to handle.

24th

Yesterday the main t'gallant staysail halyard broke as did the chain sheet for the main royal. I have spent what seems like many hours trying to repair the halyard but one mishap after another seems to occur. The blocks needed switching and the splice needed serving.

It has been good to busy myself but a quiet desperation remains with me always.

What will I do after this? Can I bear to go home? Where is home? If home is where the heart is, I shall never reach it for my heart is in all around. Everything and nothing possesses it. A warm wind from the North east surges us on to Saipan.

On Death
Can death be sleep when life is but a dream
And scenes of bliss pass as a phantom by?
The transient pleasures as a vision seem
And yet we think the greatest pain's to die.

How strange it is that man on earth should roam
And lead a life of woe, but not forsake
His rugged path; nor dare he view alone
His future doom which is but to awake.

(John Keats)

Prepare a face to meet
the faces that you meet – (TS Eliot)

Having crossed an ocean, *Europa* lay in a dry dock as if the water had dried up and the sky had filled with towering cranes, making the three masts look slightly absurd.

Turning through the dockyard, deafened by the scream of angle-grinders and constant thudding hammers I left the ship, bound for home.

[*Europa* had finally arrived in Japan. Nick helped in a refit, before coming home for a week's rest.]

Towards Korea:
The Hardest Voyage

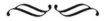

[Nicholas rejoined the ship in early May for a more crowded and taxing voyage. After the long dreamy crossing of the Pacific and the visit to Nonwin Atoll they were now doing hard business, on show, earning the ship's keep by sailing towards the World Cup year 'Sail Korea' celebrations with Korean trainees aboard. He joined on the southern island of Okinawa, for the race towards Incheon.]

May 07

Well, what can I say so far? I left my mother at Heathrow and boarded my flight on time. I am sitting in the departure lounge of Tokyo Haneda at the moment waiting for my flight to Okinawa. Everything has gone surprisingly well so far. The only thing is that I have not slept properly for 24 hours. The world takes on a not entirely unpleasant aspect through tired eyes; the airport spotlights high in the ceiling seem to thread my attention towards them. I see a drink called Pocari Sweat and laugh embarrassingly loud. Even the icily precise Japanese violin music, which would normally fall on irritated ears, creates wave-like sensations in my temples when it weaves its way periodically from the speakers of the tannoy.

At Heathrow I was agitated and now I am downright nervewracked. A voice inside my head tells me not to go back. Not to face the faces which, let's face it, I could not face when I left in Saesebo. If I am honest, there is one person who I particularly dread meeting. The person who always hangs around in the background of my dreams, incomplete, fading and resolving like a breaking wave. I must don my outer shell again for a while. It is my only chance.

May 12

There is a degree of vagueness about my recollection of the past few days. I attempted to walk from Okinawa airport to *Europa*, but set off two miles in the wrong direction, sweating and heaving my backpack. I ended up taking a taxi for what would have been a ridiculously short walk had I known the way. I had slept through the entire flight and thus had no idea exactly where Okinawa was. I had expected a similar climate to Tokyo, and so had a fright when the wave of heat broke over me upon stepping off the plane. I was much further south than I thought I would have been.

Boarding *Europa* at about 7 o'clock, buzzing from caffeine and the introduction of company, I asked how everything had been on the ship. There was not a lot of news but, as it turned out, I had gone on board only half an hour before a band of Korean trainees. I quickly stowed my luggage in the crew-cave, which was 35 degrees and looked as if a bomb had hit it. A foam mattress lay on the floor, shoes and towels spilt out of bags, and the usual assortment of unwanted junk was festooned on the bunks. I noticed that the bin had not been emptied since I left. My discarded jeans still lay there, like trashy guardians of time, linking my two experiences.

I determined to keep all my possessions in my bags at the foot of my bunk. I felt strongly tempted to piss all around it to mark my territory. I made my way on deck and had a few quick subliminal conversations with my old friends. Next, I took a stroll around the other ships in the military dock area. One which particularly caught my eye was the 'Kaisae'. This was a brigantine rigged ship but it struck me as strange. It had the hull of a yacht and a square rig. I wondered what must have been under the waterline to support the weight of that rig. Perhaps if I was less anti-social I would have asked. But I did not.

Returning from my stroll, I saw the Koreans boarding the ship, cameras out and nearly all with voluminous amounts of luggage. Marianne and the new cook's assistant Jenni had prepared some food for them, and I hope that they felt welcome. I well remember how I was on coming on board a strange ship, and remember how welcome I was made. Despite my tiredness I tried to be cheerful and welcome them in the same friendly way.

After another short walk I found myself very ready to crash into a graceless repose. Remember, it was a hot day, and the ventilation for the crewcave is, for some reason, buried deep inside a locker. I lay there soaking, marinading in sweat until the imaginative events of my mind began to take over and I slid into an oblivious sleep. Just before I was completely asleep, a surge of mental energy made me recall that I should have contacted my parents. I am not sure to this day whether I dreamt that I spoke to them or whether I spoke to them.

I was woken up at 0730 on the 10th, and with a feeling bordering on relief I clambered out of my pit. A friend of mine once described tropical sleeping conditions on *Europa* as 'Like sleeping in a dog's mouth'. I felt this description to be worthy of poetry.

After a light breakfast, for the heat had diminished my appetite, I asked about the ship's maintenance. Being away from the ship for even a short time really takes you out of the loop. I had no idea what needed doing. Rick was kind enough to give me a job on the heading which occupied my time nicely until coffee break. Thank God for chafing. It has filled many otherwise bleak hours.

At about 1100, Reinoud, crewmember and *Europa* office guru, asked me to lend a hand with some basic training aloft for the young Koreans. I say young, however most of them were aged 20–25. Their understandable timidity made them seem younger. I took up about nine people individually, all of whom were remarkably eager and, considering that it was their first time aloft, unafraid. I enjoy taking people aloft for their first time. The raw thrill, which I feel as only a background noise now, was present in them as they clambered round the main, waving to their friends down below. I appreciated this, and some of that pioneering feeling returned to me. The rigging became vibrant and challenging as it had been when I first sailed on *Europa* in the summer of 2000.

This completed, it was lunchtime. Again I didn't eat much, my time ashore having left me a little chubby. One of the events of the afternoon was the Open Ship. I had to help people down from the gangway to the steps, a task which would have been very simple had so many of the visitors not been manic or infirm. I helped some people down, caught others as they slid down and politely asked others not to jump with full force onto the deck.

Overall, we had about 100 visitors on board, compared with 800 (so I am told) the day before. After this, I gave some people an individual tour of the ship. They were Dutch but moved to Okinawa when the husband got a job on the military base. To be honest, I don't know what non-sailors really want to know about on a tour. The ship is truly beautiful and I am sure that this suffices in a way, but what to say to them is a mystery to me. I try to answer their questions about the ship's heritage and working functions and will happily run through its history, but what to say otherwise? I am sure that the mechanics of the anchor winch or yard bracing cannot interest them, so what? Anyway, I hope that they enjoyed the tour. I liked looking at the boat once again through the eyes of someone new.

Time wore on. One event of note: on my evening constitutional, I met some stumblingly drunk Russian sailing cadets on the way back to their ship. They asked where I was from and I said 'England'.

'Oh' said one, 'We hear many funny stories about England. Perhaps somebody will visit'. Having established that I was on another ship they said: 'Tomorrow is the race, we will crush you, we will win'.

I replied that I did not doubt this in the slightest. They then replied 'No. Friendship will win, my friend'. Had I thought of saying this, I would be ten times a better man.

Feeling fully two feet tall, I continued back to my ship. As I went to bed, I happened to glance at the board. It transpired that I had the 2–4 in the morning watch. With this in mind I went to bed.

Sure enough, at 2 o'clock, Hans the cook (who was leaving the ship) shook me awake announcing that I was on watch. As I passed him five minutes later in the corridor, he waved his arms expressively and said to me 'I did nothing'. This implied that I had to bake the bread and do some of the cleaning work. My first watch was to be a heroic one, it seemed. It was a relief to wake up Glen (who on being woken exclaimed 'YOU!' in an accusatory way) and show him how far I had got with the baking. I had been told that Glen was an excellent baker so was more than happy to leave my misshapen loaves in his professional care.

The following morning was departure day. I had gathered from overheard conversations, such is the communication system on board, that we were to leave at 1100. I omitted to mention previously that the fore skysail mast had recently been reinstated. I was subsequently sent aloft to secure it by hammering wedges into the loose metal collars. the aim of this exercise was partly to firm up the mast, and partly to straighten it up. As I write now with ten knots of wind heeling the ship over, I feel confident that the mast is secure if not totally straight. Anyway, as I was hammering in the wedges, the ship began to get under way while a US Marines brass band played us off.

Setting sail once more temporarily enthused me. I spent some time just gazing at the other ships, slowly ghosting towards the start line for the 2 o'clock start. Any gathering of tall ships is an impressive sight, especially when they are beautifully silhouetted against the Japanese coastline. Several hours later, none of the ships had moved very far from their starting positions and we found ourselves trimming the sails almost constantly, trying to squeeze every available bit of energy from the non-existent wind. This state of affairs continued for the entire night. During the 12–4 watch we were pleased to increase our speed by 1 knot to 1.2 kts over the ground. During this watch, we also began to teach the trainees how to clean the ship. Mostly they were keen to start new jobs, but not so keen to finish them.

I am sorry, I must go quickly back in time to about 1600 on this day. In order to do this I must go back again three months to Hawaii. We acquired several sails in Honolulu, courtesy of the *Falls of Clyde*, a disused cargo ship. Most of these sails are far too large for the *Europa*, and are useful only as spare canvas. One old staysail, however, fits on the outer jibstay as a racing jib, and is known to us as the BMF (Big Motherf*****er).

Forward again to 1600. John and I were instructed to fetch BMF from its storage on top of the ship's water tank. We dragged it up through two hatches and two sets of steps, noticing on the way that there was a tear in the sail. Our engineer then set about stitching it up, and after an hour had nearly finished. It was then that I noticed that two of the corners were missing, with only ragged edges where securing rings should be. Two of the sail corners were fine.

Then we realized – the sail had four corners. Staysails only have three. We had spent a lot of effort finding and repairing the wrong sail. With the assistance of somebody more knowledgeable, we retrieved the correct sail and folded the old one with much cursing. I then kicked it down the hatch and propped it up wherever it fitted. In the crew meeting the next day, the engineer asked for the name of the 'infidel' who left a sail on top of the ship's salt-water pump. I owned up, hoping finally to close the episode.

Anyway, the 12th dawned, as I slept peacefully. I woke in a daze and slowly became conscious during breakfast. The wind had picked up very slightly, and there was a slight angle of heel. By lunchtime, the wind was a high F3 and I had spent half an hour balancing on the skysail repairing a sheet which had broken. In the process of furling, Rick ripped the sail slightly so that it could not be re-set. *Europa's* skysails are so delicate as to be almost ethereal: vapour-like hangings which fill in the slightest breeze and tear in the merest. By the time I had re-attached the sheet, which had been frayed right through in the cheek-block, I was ready to be thoroughly sick. I could not even manage a small piece of bread. My queasiness and headache last to this moment.

At 1400 I came off watch and began to write this section of the account. To avoid a Tristram Shandy moment, I shall move on swiftly.

Dinner unfortunately included boiled vegetables, which got everywhere and added fully half an hour to my cleaning of the galley, which I found myself doing alone. This puts me in a rotten mindset. Nobody had volunteered to help me, they were on deck enjoyng themselves. For the first time the thought surfaced that I made a mistake in returning to *Europa*. Here I end my account of the 12th.

13th

My day began at 0400. I felt strongly energised on waking up, despite having taken a caffeine pill before I slept. Caffeine or no, I kept on waking up and seeing a shadowy figure standing over my bed, so vivid sometimes that I almost addressed it. Sometimes the figure seemed behind me or beside me during the day. I wonder who it is and what he has in mind for me.

Anyway, I came into the deckhouse and was barraged by questions from Glen. The first of these questions was what Bristol was the capital of? I replied that Bristol was just Bristol and nobody really gave a fuck. By 5 o'clock, a little of the same energy was creeping into the sky. I did not get much achieved except a grommet and a bindsel in this time. The crew responsibilities were still not posted, so I felt somewhat without direction.

The wind had died a little, so had my seasickness. I just had a headache. So when it came to be time to wash the deck I was not in the mood. Right then, and all through the day, I felt that the amount of work that I had to do was overwhelming. Maintenance, cleaning, training and galley work came up to me like a terrible brick wall. Even as I watched the sun rise, forming cloud patterns of infinite intricacy, my spirits were not lifted.

At breakfast time, I binged on peanut butter and jam sandwiches, not because I wanted them but because I could not seem to help myself. Self-control bowed to something else, an overriding urge which, although we consider it to be inferior, can dominate us all at times. Why? I do not know. I let sleep be my sanctuary for a while, an escape from the rationality of which I possess so little.

Lunchtime came around, I ate quickly and went to wash up alone for a while, before the people and the noise came to disturb my reverie. The 2 o'clock meeting once again reminded me of the sheer amount of work which lay before me, and the wall into which I was sailing became visible again. The crew responsibilities were posted and I was placed on jib-boom and garbage maintenance. Crappy jobs in many respects. The garbage has to be stored and accounted for on a regular basis, a gargantuan job on a ship of 40 people in waters where very little can be disposed of overboard.

The birthday routine for Jenni was done. It is always nice to celebrate a birthday on board. The decorations are retrieved and a brief sense of festivity fills the air. As I write, songs are being sung and Hans is thrumming away for our trainees, who seem to be very happy indeed. I wonder what it must be like to have a birthday on board. Does the fabric of time ripple slightly for you on that day, or does the routine of the ship continue to overwhelm you in its path? I should like to find out but am glad not to know.

Anyway, I began what was to be a pleasant watch with the obs. at 1430. The temperature has held steady at just under 25 degrees, as has the weather as a whole. Next, I finished re-swaging the outer jib to its hanks on the stay. When we were setting the BMF, Erika accidentally began to remove the outer jib, making this job necessary. She has been ill these past few days and is not improving.

After the coffee break, I assisted Seth and Marianne in sorting out the freezer. We inventoried and tidied it, a cold job but strangely fun due to the lack of mental application it required. The next task was to rig the studding-sail gear. I took a nervous trainee with me and left him on the upper topsail yard while I went aloft to reach for the broken hisail halyard. The rigging went unexpectely smoothly and by dinner time, two hisails were filling on the yards. The trainee found himself unable to step onto the course yard due to the distance. I profoundly admire the way in which he endeavoured to do so. He has the makings of a better sailor than myself.

After dinner, I had a cigarette with John. He is conscious of 'slowing down'. This is his last passage on board *Europa* and I do not blame him for wanting to leave. He thoroughly deserves the rest.

14th

So ... whose day begins at midnight with the task of telling young Koreans how to clean out a toilet? Mine does. I awoke, yet again, and it is almost fruitless to say so but being dragged from rest is an impacting thing. In 'Endymion' and 'Sleep and Poetry' Keats expounds upon the virtues of sleep. I maintain that it is as far from being idle as we can be, by its very antithesis of physical activity. The forcible release of mind has become inestimably important to me. This, reading and writing, are my few releases.

Erika's absence could really be felt in the co-ordination of the cleaning. I slowly took down the birthday decorations and began to clean the corridor and deck-house. When teaching trainees to clean, my only aim is to make the oven look better than it did before. I leave the cleaning to those with suitable levels of mental application. As watches go, the first watch of the day was uneventful. Towards the end, I found myself deliberately filling time in pointless ways, lingering over minute tasks yet leaving them somehow unfinished. I finally settled for doing wakeups, and was chided by many for not telling people that it was raining when I woke them. To tell the truth, I had hardly noticed that it was raining. Being the only one in a T-shirt when most were in thermals seemed to surprise most people. My thoughts make me oblivious to the wet and cold. Physical discomfort is often a mental reflection on outward circumstances rather than a physical reaction to them. So when the complaints came flooding in, I did not fully understand the reason for them. They washed over me like the rain washed over them. The ship was proceeding well, with both hi-sails still set.

Now I come to a troubling episode. Perhaps not troubling for the observer or reader, but for me. I dreamt last night of diseases, unleashed by my own self and malice at creating them. I awoke, firmly believing that I was covered in toxic spores which it was more than my life was worth to inhale. I could not breathe. The obvious solution came to me. I had to jump into the water, thus washing the spores off, then once under water I could breathe again. I reached the companionway steps, thankfully unseen, in just my boxer shorts before I realized that it was a dream. I promptly went back to bed and before long began to realize that it was not a dream. However, waking rationality had diluted the fantasy and I only believed that I would be ill if I inhaled. People were shouting at me, accusing me of deeds which I did not know that I had committed until that moment. I woke to see the dark figure standing by me again.

15th

I regret that I did not continue my account of yesterday when the opportunity was there. At 5.30 in the afternoon, events made my plan to continue writing at midnight almost impossible. I shall briefly resume yesterday's account, although the nature and frequency of subsequent events makes it difficult. The outstanding feature of the morning watch was the fire drill. I had no idea that the drill was scheduled, so when the alarm sounded I assumed that it was false. I then heard the intercom announcement that we should check the forepeak and bilges. I went into the forepeak and saw no fire so came up, grabbed the breathing suit and made my way aft. By this time the bemused trainees were being shoved on deck by some of the crew. The alarm had not sounded for very long and many had not grasped that this was a fire drill. Some were even attempting to sneak back down below to finish their breakfasts. We distributed lifejackets among them while the fire team searched in vain for the non-existent fire. Unlike the previous three drills, I did not embarrass myself and the drill as a whole seemed to go well.

Later in the watch, the wind rose slightly and all stunsail gear was removed. The skies were grey and the drizzle constant but I stayed in my shorts and T shirt, not feeling the cold which others seemed to feel. When I finally went to bed, the ship was moving along well in moderate conditions.

I slept, but as usual in a disturbed manner. At about five-thirty I became conscious of the ship suddenly heeling over at a far greater angle than before. The two bells which signify 'all crew on deck' did not need to ring (although ring they did) for me to get dressed and rush up to deck level. Once again I was wearing shorts and T shirt, so was given a shock when I squeezed out through the huddle of trainees into bitter cold wind and rain searing across the ship. I joined in furling the sails for as long as I could before I ran down to look for my jacket. I scrambled through the tangle of jackets until the flash of yellow that was mine appeared. Rushing out again I could feel the rising wind and see drops of water being broken loose from the surface of the sea as we crashed down the rising waves, ludicrously overpowered.

In the process of furling sail, we broke several buntlines and at least one downhaul. The tack on the main course also parted, thankfully with few repercussions. Stowing a sail aloft when it is without its buntlines can be very daunting. The canvas flogs with far more power than usual, threatening to tear the sail to shreds. Furling becomes almost an act of violence .

[this fuller account of the gale was written later, in harbour]

When the wind blows with force through the rigging of a ship, the taut stays and closely packed straining lines vibrate together and give off a strange, whistling note. As the ship lunges and plunges through the waves below, the note varies to form an erratic melody. For a sailor in the rig, the sound dominates all others, placing him in a different world to the spray-flecked and lively deck. Down on the deck itself it is a faint but persistent trill, less noticeable but a constant reminder of the gigantic forces which act upon our little ship. For 24 hours this note is to be heard from the rigging of *Europa*.

In the hours before the gale the skies had been grey and the visibility marred by a persistent drizzle which hung in drops from every line, block and sailor on board in a way which driving rain never does. Although we were within the Japanese archipelago the giant meteorological forces of the Pacific were operating upon us. The wind did not rise gradually, over the course of hours, but suddenly in a second as the ship collided with a wall of air, a slope down which air was rushing from the clouds.

I was falling asleep when it hit and felt the ship start to heel over as if it had been punched. Two bells rang 'all hands on deck', signifying the end of the off-watch's rest. The warm sanctuary of the cabin was replaced by the howling tangle of the deck. Lines which had been slack fearless objects a few minutes before were thrashing and straining with all the power of the wind. Neat coils of rope were thrown to the deck creating snakelike tangles as people struggled into oilskins and harnesses ready to reduce sail. Klaas was in the thick of things as he shouted orders, calculating and refining while wind and rain played in his hair like a tattered sail. The Mate was standing at the wheel, sending the ship downwind, overpowered like the sea from which the wind was dislodging a fine spray, slowly gripping and turning into waves.

Steering a tall ship is often a task of minor importance, requiring only half one's attention, but now, if the mate was doing it it had become the second most important job on the ship. One mistake at the helm could lead to the ship rounding up, letting an acre of canvas flog itself to pieces. Or the ship could fall off a wave, becoming dislodged from the rhythmic gimbals on which she seemed to be so finely balanced.

Emerging on deck to this scene was one of life's wild moments. The wind was stronger, the waves were larger and the lazy to-and-fro of slack ropes had become a struggling thrash. As gear reaches its limit and begins to break, the familiar rigging becomes a forbidding web set inharmoniously against the sky. The question must have arisen in all our minds 'When will it stop?', 'when will the wind stop rising?'.

Common sense has an answer, but it is absorbed in following orders, climbing the sodden rigging and balancing the ship with the new forces which are propelling it. As feet felt for the footropes and nervous hands clutched the yardarms high above the deck, Klaas became like the conductor of an orchestra, modifying the discordant rhythms of *Europa* into a harmony with the wild and barren sea.

The chaotic deck gradually fell back into order. Ropes were re-fastened and re-hung, safety nets were set up for the waves which were already beginning to sweep the deck. By night the waves are invisible and the rogue, swamping giant that takes you off your feet comes in silently from a rain-tinted blackness. Those frantic first moments had vanished like the sail which lay below the yards, caught calmly up in rough bundles.

As our 5th day at sea drew to a close the wind lost its biting edge, the waves doffed their white caps and a foggy calm descended upon us. I mistook the impression left on *Europa* by the strong winds of the 14th for a fleeting one.

It was like a dream where every aspect of normal life is magnified, every benign feature made razor-sharp and menacing. In the daytime you drop a glass, and that night its shattering shatters your whole world. So it is with a gale. The missed footing or unsecured line has an enhanced and deathly significance.

[return here to the onboard log]

After about an hour and a half, we had most of the sails furled and the situation under control. I was still in my shorts and shivering miserably as a result, while the on-watch rigged safety nets along the side of the ship. I ate dinner, got into some warm dry clothes and prepared for a long night. During the 8–12 watch, we set a few more sails and were simply on standby for most of the time, lest the wind should squall again.

When I got off watch I tried to get some sleep. Anxiety, combined with the motion of the ship, made it impossible. And I lay in my bunk wondering why I was here and not at home, happy, warm and comfortable.

The next watch was a busy one. Damage had to be repaired, sails set and then furled again almost instantly when the wind rose, putting our gunwales underwater from time to time. I seemed to end up with a thousand small tasks to complete and no time at all in which to do so. By the end of the watch I was so tired and hungry that even simple tasks seemed to be beyond me. I recall trying to untwist a 40-inch length of rope which was to be used as a new buntline, and getting it hopelessly tangled while onlookers laughed at me. I gave up on this project quickly and ate breakfast. I ate as if I was filling a ravine. Five jam sandwiches seemed to be sucked inside me in the same way that air is sucked into a person's lungs. The same went for lunchtime. The continual motion, the cold and the knowledge of what could be required of one sap energy surprisingly quickly. This time, I did sleep.

Time trickles on, escaping me in its crafty floods. The next watch was principally a continuation of the repairs. Servings, splicings, seizings took up my time profitably.

16th.

I baked in the next watch. I had considered the operation to be a success until the 2 o'clock meeting, when the comment was made that the bread was underdone and I had left the oil and shortening in the wrong place. Nevertheless, I enjoyed the breadmaking and being helped by the trainees. According to the young one who helped me, all the guys on board say 'Nick looks like a baby but he works all the time'. I am not sure exactly what is implied by the word 'baby' in this case. The language barrier could make 'baby' simply a term for 'very young'. Either way, the phrase fascinated me deeply and also egotistically.

I woke the next morning to bacon and eggs for breakfast. I knew that I had to give a lesson at 9 o'clock on basic knots and their application. This prospect daunted me since I often make mistakes with knots myself, so teaching others could prove difficult. I had planned to prepare the ropes and what I was to say in advance, however after waking up and showing Rick how to rig the stunsail gear (for the wind has now died down considerably) I had only 5 minutes to gather up the five trainees I was to teach. In the end, I was pleased with the way that the lesson went. The trainees were keen and receptive. Being English, my idea of teaching was of the wilful forcing of information upon an unwilling subject.

We were able to cover most of the basic knots and review them in under 2 hours, thanks entirely to the 5 trainees. I enjoyed giving the lesson and I hope that they enjoyed it also. It is, of course, not being able to tie a knot just the once which teaches you how to tie a knot. It is the repeated usage in practical situations which defines it. I hope that some of the information I gave will stay.

The remainder of the watch I spent sorting out some of the ship's garbage. I had been neglecting this duty recently, mainly because of the weather and the stream of other jobs which have been coming my way as a result of it. So I spent an hour and a half crushing tin cans and sorting through chemical waste. Not such a pleasant job, but it filled the time and took me away from company, which I am avoiding at the moment for my own reasons.

At lunch I did not feel like eating much. The decreased level of activity after the last few days has left me with far less need of food than previously. After lunch came the 2 o'clock meeting where my baking failures were brought to my attention.

Here is where time past meets time present:

> I feel as if I am surrounded by a veil which isolates me from others in a perilous way. It is as if they are standing behind their clothes, irrelevant and unaware of me. I move through the ocean alone, feeling only slight brushing tendrils of others in my weaving and airless path. I long to be at home where I can study and expand, form opinions from learning, write my thoughts as and when they appear. But I know that this is not really an option for me. I have become more solipsistic than ever before, for no reason that I can recount.

In the two o'clock meeting I felt the distance growing. I somehow felt like screaming at how unmoved my own mind had become. As Tennyson put it

'I shall bury myself in myself
And the devil may pipe to his own'

17th

At the moment it is ten o'clock in the morning. I spent the early watch in the forepeak splicing and serving. At four o'clock it was bitterly cold. I wore my woolly hat for the first time since my voyage on the *Malcolm Miller* in '99. At 7.45 we were told to prepare for a tack so, without breakfast, I shivered my way through the heaving of ropes and arranging of trainees. I will remember the way in which my hands burned for quite some time to come. First, the headsails are loosed and the mizzen is hauled in to turn the ship. When the squaresails become backed, the main yards are hauled over, followed by the fore (I think).

Just when I thought that it was time for breakfast, I was sent up to the horrid skysail yards to overhaul the buntlines. This involves standing on the skysail yard from which position the buntline blocks (and the masthead) can be reached. By the time I had reached the yard itself, my hands were so cold that it took 15 minutes just to jam the ropes into the blocks so that the buntlines would not fall back out of place and crumple the sail. After I had done this, I shinned up the remaining four feet of mast and touched the top, just for posterity. I then descended to deck level as quickly as I could for some much-needed breakfast and sleep. I had just begun to eat my breakfast sandwich when Eric came into the lounge and said that we were going to anchor and that all the crew had to come on deck to assist with taking away the sails.

I said goodbye to the idea of a quiet breakfast and tramped on deck. We took in the sails and I tried to have a peaceful smoke, but no. Now the engineers told me that I had been stacking the garbage incorrectly and I will soon be rearranging it. Reinoud then berated me about something which I had sometime done something wrong with. I do not know when I shall be able to sleep ever again.

It is now evening. I must admit that soon after my last paragraph I fell soundly asleep until lunchtime. I was woken up by Lisette and I thought that I was being attacked. Lisette remarked upon the violence with which I leapt up, thankfully finding it funny. What is perhaps less funny is that my hand went to my knife. She did not see this and within seconds my sense of the rational returned, and I calmed down. The smell of lunch and familiar surroundings replaced the daunting place which I inhabited for those few seconds.

I ate, or should I say binged, on pizza and peanut-butter sandwiches and felt better for it. Better able to face yet another watch feeling lonely, surrounded by wetly clinging mist, waiting for the order to tack or work in the rigging. The wind then died away completely and the tide had turned against us. The finishing line is only 11 miles off but we were being gradually swept away from it, seemingly further into the bubble of mist and complete obscurity. The decision was then taken to anchor until – I am sorry, this was earlier and I have already recorded it. Please ignore the last two thirds of this paragraph, or mentally place it where it belongs.

The entire crew were quietly drinking coffee and standing by to raise the anchor and set sail, in order to finish the race. I volunteered to stow the anchor chain, and climbed into some overalls, ready for the moment. Unfortunately the battery for the winch start-motor was old and drained, this delaying by one and a half hours the raising of the anchor.

When it was finally there, I squeezed myself down into the anchor chain locker, taking with me an extra working light, for the light in the locker always seemed insufficient to illuminate the eerie corners of that hole. I left above the hatch a Korean trainee, with instructions to call for the anchor winch to be stopped should yells of agony be heard from within the locker. The anchor chain, although fed fairly slowly, is heavy and unforgiving, with plenty of opportunity for hair and fingers to become wedged in between the links. The chain locker itself is a cramped space right at the bottom of the ship, with a single halogen light casting shadows over the expanses of neatly laid anchor chain. The ship has two separate anchor chains, the port chain considerably shorter and seldom used to my knowledge. The chains are separated by a metal sheet divide. In order for the chain to be stowed singlehanded, it is necessary for one to slide on top of the unused chain. Scrabbling into position, I thought how similar the locker must be to an old-fashioned mine. I found that just being on top of the anchor chain was nerve-wracking. It takes a less vivid imagination than mine to imagine what would happen if the chain clutches were to fail while I was perched on top.

The anchor winch began and I started to lay the chain out in the criss-cross configuration. It took about thirty minutes to complete the operation, by which time I was sweating, despite the cold of the locker and the even colder seawater and grime on the chain. I was interested to note that when I held my filthy hands up to the light, steam was rising from them, as if smoke was seeping through my skin, such was the temperature difference between me and the air around. I felt a distinct sense of relief when I heard the anchor-winch engine die away and could crawl out, dirty but satisfied, all claustrophobia annihilated.

I have avoided this far using the word claustrophobia simply because it denotes an irrational fear of small spaces. A fear of this particular small space is the very antithesis of an irrational fear.

In the same way that opposites attract, I was then deployed onto the skysail yard for the second time that day to overhaul the buntlines. I found, this time, to my satisfaction that the lines could be more effectively overhauled simply by jamming them between the yard and the sail, thus saving myself a short but potentially hazardous climb.

Most of the afternoon watch was spent in setting and adjusting sail. At about six o'clock, a ship became faintly visible through the fog. It turned out to be the *Kaisei*, heading like us for the finish line. Being the faster ship, it gradually gained ground on us until a shouted dialogue between the Korean trainees on both ships grew up and became fairly lively. Eventually she bore off and disappeared into the fog, re-emerging having tacked across our bows about an hour later. We were subsequently told to prepare for a tack, completed after dinner which I was in no mood to eat.

When the activities were completed I took up my usual place under the forepeak awning for a cigarette when I was joined by John and then by Rick and Erika. I left the three of them to talk and I do not believe that they were sorry to see me leave.

18th

As days on board the *Europa* go, irregularity has characterized the day. I woke up, by some chance, at midnight, rushed into my clothes and ran on deck, mentally cursing the infidel who had failed to wake me. Arriving on deck, I found that Seth was the only other person awake from my watch. It turned out that we had anchored an hour earlier and were on an anchor-watch system. My getting up had volunteered me for two hours of cleaning the ship. I directed three of the trainees to assist me and within an hour, most of the cleaning was done and I could send them back to their bunks. The silent generator was running so the ship was eerily silent. The masthead lights were barely visible through the shrouds of thick fog. It was like the bleakest image of divine light that can be imagined. Also, the cold damp air seemed to cling to every surface of the ship, making brass-polishing next to impossible. At two o'clock Rick and Erika were woken and I went to bed, expecting to be roused again at 4 o'clock to weigh anchor. However, it was not until 6.30 that the crew was shaken. We set sail in about twenty minutes, then trimmed for another thirty. Breakfast seemed like a godsend.

The wind was slight, and although we had only six and a half miles to go, it did not look as if we were going to make it. I spent most of the watch aloft, stitching closed a tear in the main t'gallant staysail. I stitched from a seat on the crosstrees which seemed ideal at first, until I had to stand up an hour later and found that I quite literally could not move my legs. It took about ten minutes of doing a contorted little jig on the crosstrees, watched by several amused trainees.

Beside this, the sail corner was so rotten that it could be torn between finger and thumb. I did not even need a palm to get the needle through. The whole exercise was virtually pointless. I came down briefly before lunchtime to get some more thread and was told off by Reinoud for not having read the ISM manuals. I then realized, not for the first time, that there are many aspects to being a crewmember about which I just don't care. I do not care about safety procedures, which pins fit which blocks and the like. This is why I will never be a good crewmember. That is why I should leave before I start spreading discontent. I feel like a virus.

We crossed the finish line about about two o clock this afternoon.

From five o'clock, my day has considerably gathered in interest.

The sun came out for the first time in a week and everybody seemed to be enjoying themselves. Then we had a man-overboard drill. The alarm sounded and we hove to. Heaving to simply involves bracing the mainmast aback. In the process of this operation a clewline broke on the course, sending a block skimming down to the deck on its line. The sloopie [ship's boat] was lowered down quickly on the davits and the casualty, which took the form of a plastic buoy, was brought on board on the brancard [stretcher]. This was the end of the drill.

Since the boat was proceeding slowly under sail and the weather was now perfect, some of the trainees and crew were taken out in the sloopie to take photographs. I had never seen the ship looking so utterly beautiful as she did from the outside today. In the dimming light, the sails took on a gold-tinged aspect as the hull cut through the water smoothly sailing to her anchorage. I felt in that time that perhaps I was in the right place for that moment. Some of the misery of the past few days was washed away as I watched the ship on which I had crossed two oceans making her stately way onwards. Such strength and such peace, perfectly combined. This was not the ship of buzzing alarms. It was the romanticism of the ship of the past, embodied for me to see for a few brief moments.

I brought the sloopie along to the davits with some difficulty. The ship was now moving almost as fast as the little boat could do. After getting her in place and the lines fixed the sloopie was hauled into its davits with John and me hanging on to the safety lines.

As I write, the ship is at anchor amongst the other tall ships. The sails are furled and the rest of the crew are having a good time. I talked to some of the Korean girls for a while but I do not feel like joining the fray above. My place is alone with my thoughts right now. I feel it profoundly.

[Nick wrote more formally, for the website, an account of the arrival after the gale. It seems of interest by way of contrast, to see how a voyage can be blandly described when the personal struggle and exhaustion is airbrushed out ...]

Trainees and permanent crew together worked to repair all the minor damage in double quick time. Even when the motion of the ship was at its greatest John was not prevented from producing 4 delicious loaves of bread for the next morning. Some felt understandably tired after the exertions of the previous 24 hours, but we were all closer because of it. In the rough patches especially, everybody on board must pull together to make the ship run smoothly. In turn, everybody is pulled together by the ship.

Our 17 young Korean trainees were now keener than ever to learn more about life at sea: we gave them lessons about basic sail handling, rope work, terminology and recognizing other types of ships. As we tentatively set our magnificent studding sails, the trainees started to become more familiar working aloft in the rigging. The ship glided on with grace and comfort, with everybody now able to lend a helping hand to its running. A feeling of content spread to all on board as we made our way towards the welcoming arms of Incheon. We were happy sailors.

By the morning of the seventh day out of Okinawa, the wind turned against us and died away to the vaguest whisper. Tendrils of fog hung around the ship in a moist shroud. The square sails hung limply from the yards and the ship was propelled by tidal forces alone. We were a mere 11 miles from the finishing line but the tide was turning against us, sweeping us away from our goal. Our strange yet effective racing tactic was to drop the anchor until the tide was favourable. The sails were struck and we waited. By the afternoon we had a breath of wind and some current under us. With full sail close hauled we began once again to slice through the thick curtain of fog. At this point, a shape began slowly to emerge from astern. We had become used to sharing the sea with Korean fishing vessels and their liberally distributed nets, but as the shape drew closer it showed itself to be our competitor ship the brigantine *Kaisei*. Slowly, she pulled out of the mist and, being the faster ship, began to gradually overtake us.

She passed so close that a lively conversation could be held in Korean between their trainees and ours. Spirits soared and brief stories were exchanged before she tacked into the mist and vanished just as she had appeared. 2 hours later she was seen again for a brief moment when she crossed our bow. She had tacked ahead of us. The bubble of mist in which we had existed in solitude had been temporarily inhabited by this beautiful ship.

As the day ran on we were forced to anchor against the current one more time. We spent a morning squeezing out every drop of speed that we could, manipulating the smallest shift in the wind to make it to the finish line. At 2 minutes past 2 o'clock in the afternoon, we crossed the line to much rejoicing by all. As if in sympathy with our mood, the fog unfurled itself from around the ship and the sun appeared. Sweaters and waterproofs were replaced by T-shirts and shorts as we made our final approach to the anchorage.

The ship's tender 'Sloopie' was lowered into the water at 5 o'clock as the retrieval boat for man overboard drill. Since the weather was excellent and the sea was calm, the trainees and some of the crew took a short trip in 'Sloopie' to see *Europa*, under sail, from the outside. Some of the crew who had been on board for many months had never seen *Europa* sailing from the outside perspective. The sunlight was just starting to fade and the ship was bathed in golden light. The outward beauty of *Europa* had been with us every day, but we had not been able to see it until this moment.

We anchored again in the clear evening light. The next few days were spent on anchor and we used the time to prepare the ship for entry into Incheon. We cleaned her inside and out, decks were swabbed and paintwork touched up. Even the scuppers, into which sea and rainwater drains from the deck, were given a shiny new coat of paint.

[We return now to the daily journal.]

19th

A cleaning day. I ate little and subsisted on caffeine pills. I remember very little of the day. Shaking hand makes it difficult to write or think at all right now.

20th

As you may have gathered from my last entry, yesterday was a bad day for me. We spent the entire day at anchor, cleaning and working. At nine o'clock I gave up on the day and went to bed. Today has been far more interesting. I was not woken and therefore missed breakfast. Feeling weak therefore, I came up on deck, drank coffee, pretended to work and waited for us to weigh anchor and sail into Incheon harbour.

Getting underway was good fun. Setting sail brought back some of the life in the ship which was so badly lacking yesterday. I took one of the Korean girls aloft with me to unfurl the royal. She had never climbed so high before and to my mind showed extreme gallantry in what cannot have seemed an easy task.

One incident I would like anachronistically to record is my anchor watch from 0400 to 0600 on the 19th. Lisette had made about six kilos(!) of beautifully rolled cookie dough, which I was told to cut and bake. I must confess that baking is my weak point. Only a few days earlier I got a complaint from Klaas that the bread I made was underdone. I was nervous about cutting up and baking these cookie rolls which were evidently prepared with great love and attention. The baking turned out alright, with the help of the Korean trainee who was stationed to help me.

I had to check on the bridge regularly, checking for ships approaching in the thick morning fog. On one of these perennial little checks the distress light came up on the DSC radio receiver and an alarm sounded. Somewhere, not a million miles away, a ship was in trouble. I wondered what was happening on that ship, whether men were frightened, climbing into liferafts on an empty sea or jammed against an unforgiving rock. My reverie was shattered by the appearance of the captain stomping out in just his underwear, switching off the radio and returning to bed.

We sailed past the gently wooded Korean rocks and islands which marked our approach to the coast. Being the only ship in sight under sail, I felt a being in distinct contrast to the approaching city and passing dayboats. The sun was shining and our progress was stately. A police boat dropped by and, to the delight of the trainees, gave the ship a tub of a spring vegetable mix called 'Kim chi'. This was later prepared by some of the trainees in the galley and was delicious.

We were told that we would not be entering the harbour today and were to anchor again. I had the 10 till midnight anchor watch, which was pleasant. People were still cooking, moving about and talking in the deckhouse so I did not have to clean it. One of the games that they played was this: every member of the group had to tell what they were doing at a certain age. In passing, I was asked what I was doing at age 17. I reflected on the bleakness of this time for me. My first trip on board *Europa* is the outstanding memory from this time: the rest is work and anti-depressants. I am thankful that this is behind me and hope that my future madness will take a more lively form.

With half-formed thoughts shaping and dissolving in my head, I went to bed. Again, nobody woke me the next day and I had to rush to catch breakfast. My work for a majority of the day was cut out by Seth, who asked me to re-bindsel the main middle staysail onto its ring-hanks. This seemed to be a short job but handling the sailcloth was like trying to fold a stapled cardboard box. When the head and foot were finally attached, I decided to hoist the staysail bit by bit and do the bindsels one by one. The wind was very slight throughout the day, so this was not a problem. It took most of the day to complete the task. Many times I had to lower myself from my perch on a bottlescrew and climb down to the deck to loosen a halyard or drink a cup of coffee, which was readily available on deck. At lunch I ate six sandwiches in quick succession and cursed myself for it.

I am beginning to find the routine wearing. We are never really off watch or on watch. For instance, people stop really working at 5 o'clock but if one person continues to work, everybody else feels guilty and slowly continues to work also. Furthermore, tonight we are supposed to go into harbour at 11 o'clock. This means another interrupted night. The 12 hour days continue in harbour also. It is becoming like drudgery. A lot of work, very little sailing and no real chance to see the country which we travelled very far to see.

At 1230 in the evening, we were finally allowed to enter the lock along with *Kaisei* and by 0230 were docked. The crew of the New Zealand ship *R. Tucker Thompson* was on the quayside to greet us and many small reunions were had on the pier. Most, if not all, of our crew had a drink with the crew of the *Tucker Thompson*.

23rd

I now skip ahead to the night of the 22nd, John's last night. The Korean trainees took us out to eat at a Korean restaurant. On entering, we were told to remove our shoes and place them at the door. At first I was a little wary since the door was open to the street. On entering, I noticed that there were no chairs and very low tables. People were sitting cross-legged on cushions at the tables. We were invited to sit down and a burner full of hot coals was placed into a hole in the table. Then the food was brought by the trainees, a plethora of colours and tastes which proved to be truly delightful.

We were induced to drink many shots (I counted 15 at the close of the evening) of a distilled rice wine called 'soju'. This had the effect of blurring everything, making time and food slip by. Everything was delicious. I ate such varieties and quantities that I quite lost count. We sang, we drank, we smoked. It was the best evening that I have had in a long time. The drudgery, broken sleep and monotony of the past few days was all forgotten to me, and the trip seemed as if it had been worthwhile after all.

The next morning we said our goodbyes to John and I watched him walk away from *Europa* with sadness, and a little envy.

[Again Nick wrote the official website account of the festival:]

The next day saw the beginning of the port festivities. All the ships were placed right in the centre of the action, just a few hundred yards away from the main stage, where performances took place throughout the day and into the night. The Korean navy stunned us with regimented displays, and the music ranged from Korean traditional to marching band music. Thousands of people thronged the wharf: the stage was alive with costumed dancers displaying an incredible richness of Korean culture echoing through the ages. Crew competitions were held: most notable was the crew singing contest, won by our musical engineer Hans who played a song of his own composition called 'Suave tune'.

Then the crew parade. *Europa*, as usual, contributed its own individual Dutch touch to the proceedings by dressing the crew in pirate costume and ingeniously constructing an ornamental ship from a few sticks and a shower curtain.

In almost every port farewells must be said. We lost John, who joined the ship 5 months ago in Panama City and only ever intended to stay on to Hawaii. But there were tearful partings too with the young Koreans: in only a short space of time they had become a part of the crew. The date for departure approached again; Barend Visser paid the ship a short visit from her headquarters in The Hague, bringing with him some new skysails, ready to fling her back onto the seas.

[The email home]

Hi Mum,

Just to let you know that I have arrived safely in Incheon. Of course, the office would contact you if I was not. You will hear from me later on so do not worry.   Nick.

[Back to the daily journal:]

26th

For the past few days I have been plagued with exhaustion. After watch, I simply collapsed into my bunk. I shall therefore briefly account for my salient memories from the past few days. On the night of John's dinner, in which my out-of-control chopsticks had sent some pig's intestine skyward, I was, being English, invited to play soccer against the Russian cadets. I was disgustingly drunk and barefoot. The Russians were icily sober and wearing combat boots. I remember as the ball scudded towards me over the ground and made contact with my feet, my swimming head sent me toppling over and I half walked, half crawled back to my ship. Luckily, by this point I was sober enough to carry on a conversation with Barend, the owner.

Another memory of this time is of Su-A. Su-A had a crush on me and during John's night had clung to me often. Although my lack of interest was clear, it did not stop her from giving me several small token gifts. This was both sweet and embarrassing.

Another time was the 25th. The day in which I took the bus into Seoul. I awoke with a fearful headache but since the alternative to the day out was another day of work on board the ship, I gladly went along. The plan was to take the crew by bus into Seoul and then split, spend the day and return by Metro. This we did. The bus went to a park, from where myself, Rick and Reinoud caught the metro to Seoul City hall. Once again, I was reminded of the difference between North Korea and South Korea. South Korea is a fully developed country. The Metro system is infinitely more advanced than the British system and stepping out onto the streets themselves proved to be a wonderful sight. It is as if the ultra-modern city of Seoul has grown up around the old Buddhist vines of temples and beautiful architecture.

We wandered around the winding backstreets which meander alongside the main arteries of the city, looking for somewhere to eat lunch. We found a small, dicy looking café which served 'salad'. The proprietor did not speak a word of English but we were welcomed in to the empty little cave all the same. First off, we were served with some strange grape-juice like wine in plastic cups. A reconstituted bottle of the stuff (which was not at all unpleasant) was also placed on the table. Then a gas burner was lit in the middle of the table and the food was placed upon it. Various types of meat and uncooked noodles, vegetables, etc were placed in the water which began to boil. The effect was to make a thick and pleasant soup-like substance which we mixed with kimchi and some tofu. Eating the whole thing with chopsticks was a messy but fun process. I am sure that the owner thought us animals. Me especially, since my place setting resembled a slaughterhouse floor by the end.

After lunch, we strolled through a fairly crowded marketplace selling what I imagine were false western goods. I say fairly crowded, for Seoul did not give me the impression of being an overcrowded city in the same way that London or New York might. It is busy and active, yet somehow not stiflingly so.

For me, the highlight of the day was the visit to the Buddhist temple. I am ashamed to say that I know little of Buddhist culture. The temple, however, stood alone, awe-inspiring. Predominantly wooden in construction, the carvings below the traditional parabolic roof framed the open front, where people within could be seen at prayer. A slim statue of Buddha stood as the centrepiece and many hundreds of candles shed their light below. A slow chant filled the timeless construction as people took to their knees, one by one, apparently as their own spiritual state directed them.

I left the temple with my mouth dry and a head bursting with thoughts. After a cup of coffee and a visit to an internet cafe, it was time to rejoin the subway system and make my way back to Incheon (Not Inchon, which is an entirely different place). The Seoul metro system is very well organized and clear, making my trip back to Domincheon a simple one (provided that I did not accidentally disembark in Tonincheon or Bonincheon).

I really wish that I could say the same of the bus service. I arrived at 6.45, which should have been plenty of time to get back for my watch at 8 o'clock. I had been told to get on bus 12. Not a difficult task in itself, but the first bus I tried to board did not work out. The driver irritably waved me off the steps. He did not want the trouble of some tourist asking volleys of questions, as I surely would. When I refused to move he reached over and with the lightest yet most accomplished shove, sent me skittering back onto the street. Indignant and with a little pride-devil enjoining risks, I determined to make a second attempt. The second driver beckoned me on board. By this time, there was no question of my being on time for my watch. I knew it, I knew even as I boarded the bus that it was the wrong one. But I was tired and thought it would be better to ride the bus, which cost next to nothing, than stand around confusing myself. The buses were, in fact, so cheap that I am sure a good night's sleep could be had on one for far less than the cost of the fine for street-sleeping.

I digress. After an hour, I admitted to myself that this bus was not going anywhere special, least of all to Incheon harbour wharf 5. Any question of being back for the watch was gone. I began to ponder where I might be, and what these places meant to the rest of the people on the bus. People had come and gone, yet some were staying. This must mean that the bus had still further to go on its journey before it began the second half of its circuit, otherwise the people would have got on the bus going in the other direction. That was assuming the bus went in a circuit. Perhaps it simply kept on rolling and rolling and ...

I had gone to sleep for about half an hour. Just myself and an old couple remained on the bus. There were no English signs, nobody spoke English, the street outside had lost the capital city neon glow. I got out. I had to do something. Once again, the Korean metro saved my life. I came upon a station and noticed to my horror that I was a long way from where I wanted to be. 45 minutes metro ride took me back to Donincheon. My watch had been over for over an hour now. This time, I got on a bus going in the opposite direction and soon the route became familiar.

I arrived back at the ship, shattered and pale, whereon I was informed by Glen that my new watch was in 25 minutes and I had to do the baking. Had I not been so stunned, I would have cried. Had it not been for the kindness of one Korean man and his care, I would have still been orbiting South Korea in a dingy bus. Thank you, Korea, thank you numbness.

29th

Again, I have not written. There is very little requirement to record the events of my sickness in any detail.

4th

The festival in Mokpo was similar to that of Incheon. The ships were positioned near to the centre stage and a customs barrier was established along the quayside. The major difference was that, being a shallow port no deeper than 7 m, larger ships had to anchor off. My best memory will be climbing up Mount Tudal. 4 dollars can go a long way if used carefully, as I found when none of my credit cards functioned.

I woke up this morning to the sound of a screaming engine. I climbed blearily on deck and found that we had already set off. We had previously said goodbye to the trainees, including the bundle of energy Sung-Soo. I had been on watch at 11 o'clock in the evening when the new trainees arrived, friendly but baffled. Strangely eough, some of them knew me from other trainees who had come on board. They tell me that I am quite famous! One new addition is my liaison officer friend from the port of Mokpo.

Shortly after leaving the dock, we were motoring through the beautiful Korean coastal islands. Combined with the thin but consistent mists, one gets the impression of walking through a curtain to get in and out of Korea. The mist is the darkness you feel and the islands are the physical brushing sensation which slows you down softly, monopolizing your senses.

I was sleepy and full of coffee when rig training began. The start of the race was at 4 o'clock, seemingly long after Mount Tudal was replaced by the transient cloud mountains. I took up Hok-shee, an energetic guy who could project humour through his own joyful weavings, even when boldly sitting atop the skysail yard. I cannot help but be impressed with how active and outgoing everybody has been. So un-British, in such a good way. As the ships gathered for the start, the classic scene was set. The starting horn echoed the minutes while ships drifted slowly toward the line. We tacked, we wore, until finally the boat began to break through the threads of mist, binding us no longer as the glassy calm received a festive sparkling from the Aeolian artists. The sun set. Tired, I close my account for today.

5th

A dog start to the day. A windless dog-watch, that is. For 2 hours I kept a fruitless watch from the bow, my head turning with tired irritability. I had not slept because I was too tired to sleep. I felt homesick and weary of the ever-renewing drudgery, the cycle of work-eat-work-sleep which has become so definitive. It was perhaps fortunate that I was on bow watch and not down below showing trainees how to clean the floors, ceilings, walls. Towards the end of the watch we wore -ship, to little effect since the sea was glassy calm, reflecting the glow of the fishing boats far off in another sphere of consciousness. By the end all I wanted to do was sleep, where if I dreamed it would be of another place, better or worse, no matter.

In spirit better, I was woken up at 7.15 for breakfast. I did not get up until 7.45. It is nearly impossible to get up half an hour early when sleep is such a precious commodity at sea. Two stunsails were set although the wind was not at the ideal angle. I discovered at lunchtime that the ship is 5th in class and 11th overall. In short, she is in last place. The ship ghosted along in the beating sun while trainees, crew and captain scraped and prepared pins and pinrails. The large old sail known as Big Desmond was transferred from deck-swabber position to main t'gallant staysail and renamed Flying Desmond. I ate excessively at lunch, I could not help myself. The afternoon drifted by in sleep, blissful calm and deep, with hazy lazy heat lapping around me.

From 8–12 – and I should warn you that if you thought my day unremarkable this caps it off – I unwrapped sugar cubes for 2 hours. The ship has on board only individually wrapped sugar cubes and they all must be unwrapped. This job I find too insulting for trainees, who are on board only for a brief period of time, and I drifted away in thought while 8 cubes per minute fell, unpacked, into the large tub.

6th

Today was, in one dominating respect, a bad day to be on board *Europa*. The 4 till 8 in the morning watch was pleasant enough. I ate too many of the fresh doughballs, helmed, trimmed sails and managed garbage. The sun rose beautifully in the cloudless sky as the ship was held motionless. Studding sails were to no avail.

I had not intended to sleep for my entire off-watch but somehow I found myself being woken up with the cry of 'lunchtime!'. Here is the bad part. At 2 o'clock Klaas told the crew that *Europa* was in the worst state that he had ever seen her. Mess and rust, he said, upset him. He said that he was sad to be leaving the ship in such a poor state and talked of finding a new job. The subsequent cleaning was ferocious but as I stood on the helm the following thoughts came to me.

The outward state of the boat seems to be a reflection of all our moods – the routine, the lethargy, nobody pulling in quite the same direction. We work hard but the ship will never be good. I am grateful to be doing what I am doing, but often wish that I was not. There are other activities closer to my heart which occupy my mind. Every day that passes, I feel slightly closer to final collapse. My stomach hurts, my head feels vice-gripped and I feel perhaps always as if somebody is behind me, ready to make a pouncing move.

I must just go through with this. Rose will be shortly into the heat of exams and my parents have enough to worry about. Jumping ship would selfishly add to their worries. It is my genuine hope that they will hear from Barend and read my internet report, believing that I am all right and happy. Maybe things will get better with the upcoming crew change in Busan/Pusan. A return to the old times is much needed right now.

[Nick was in fact quite ill, and although he does not record it saw the ship's doctor who observed that he had lost too much weight too fast in the tropical heat and overstressed himself. Things improved.]

7th

Thank God – a better day. The dog watch threw up the chance for me to bake. My task was to use up the leftover bananas. I tried to bake banana cookies but was thwarted again by my refusal to believe the recipe book. I can follow the train of thought perfectly and see where I went wrong. The moment that the thought 'I'm sure that I'll get away with ...' enters my head, I'm on a losing streak. The recipe was for cookies using dried bananas, not overripe fresh bananas. The cookie balls melted on the tray, and because the boat was heeling, slid into a gelatinous glob at the end of the tray. I hastily drained the mixture into a high-sided tin and shoved it in the oven again just to see what would happen. The end result was actually quite pleasing. Through the day the ship had wind, but it was headwind unfortunately. I now have yet another baking scar.

Also in the dog watch, the trainees made noodles for us. In short, the mood was light. The watch concluded with a tack. Normally this operation is a drag but this time I was on the helm and through this gained a whole new perspective on tacking the ship. The first stage is to fall off five degrees to give the ship that extra bit of speed and momentum through the tack. The rudder over 10, 15, 20, 25 degrees until Eric decides on the new course. Then it is a matter of shining a flashlight into the sails, trying to ascertain the best upwind course for the ship. We were forced to settle in the end for 30 degrees. Back to Mokpo! Such is the way of the sea.

I woke with a start 15 minutes late for watch. Being breakfast-time, nobody really noticed and I was able to bolt 2 cups of coffee and splash my face with water to make myself look awake before taking the 6-hourly meteorological observations. A vast majority of the watch was spent in rigging the main t'gallant staysail halyard. This was an unpleasant job at first. The thick fog left me drenched after 10 minutes, struggling and swearing at the awkwardly slewed block at which I had been tugging. Soon, however, the sun came out, warming and clarifying the horizon. The heel of the ship and tricky halyard leads made the job difficult, but it filled the time until lunch.

The 2 o'clock meeting was of a much better nature, with everybody in a far more relaxed state of mind than yesterday.

I woke a little early, read and thought until dinner time. The 8–12 watch was fun if unproductive. We had a dessert fight in the galley, continued unpacking sugar cubes and crushing the mountain of tin cans. Sue the trainee joined in and everyone was in good spirits. Glen also continued with his croissant-baking exercise. It was nice to have this short interlude. The good times are few and far between at the moment. At midnight the race was finished at sea. The wind was slight and in the wrong direction.

Next day was spent with sails all brailed up, under engine. The crew-cave became a sauna once more. As I was about to get some sleep, the fire alarm sounded, signifying a drill. The hoses were tested and I spent a majority of my time down in the daystores pretending to check for heat. The drill concluded. I sloped off to bed at last.

13th

The journey from Pusan to Yeo-Su turned out to be ludicrously short, 100 miles of motoring. It was not, however, without its uses. Rob replaced Klaas as captain and I find his approach very refreshing. He really likes people to work independently. He also takes an active approach to training the trainees, leaping about, showing lines and really teaching.

Once again the trainees are enthusiastic and jolly. I was fortunate enough to meet up with Ini Yu-Rim and the rest in Pusan; it was like having old friends back on board. Ji-won sent some of her laminated cartoons to me. This made up in part for not being allowed any real time off. I remember my sense of humour failing fast as after a hard day's work, we all had to restock the ship because the delivery had come late. Needless to say, some of the food was handled with a heavier hand than it otherwise might have been.

Right now, sitting in Yeosu with a half day coming my way, I suppose things could be worse. ... 14 days until arrival at my destination port.

I add in parenthesis, Glen will also be leaving the ship in Yokohama. He has burnt out with the constant change between sailing and opera ...

14th

Yet another footrope servicing day. Ruth was my tutee as I sweated and struggled my way through the serving operation. In view of this, good progress was made. The major interruption to this work which saw me nearly lose my temper was the giant banner given to us to fly, advertising World Expo 2010 Yeo-Su. We braced the yards square so that the stays would have obstructed the banner. I furled it up onto the t'gallant yard like a sail, which was fine. The problem was that the wind was heavy enough to send the damn thing flying off behind the yard. I gathered in the fucker before it took me into mid-air and somehow forced it down on deck. Later on I set it between the Fok and the deck, which worked well.

Now that I come to think about it, in the last 3 weeks I have had 3 run-ins with flags. One was on the mizzen while mending the topsail. Klaas' flag became caught in a block and took time to free. The next was the Korean flag being caught in the band of the bram. I respect them as ornaments but no more. Ren did not cook dinner tonight.

16th

Well, yesterday was quite a day. It began at 0400 with harbour watch in which I parcelled and served the thimble wire splice for the port side upper topsail footrope. I slept through breakfast and generally filled time before half day began. I also slept through most of lunch. I began walking into town but was given a lift by a kind stranger. I told him that I was looking for a Visa bank. He said that he thought I had a lot of guts walking into a strange town, penniless. Anyway, I eventually found a machine that would take my card and so, with money, I set out in search of anything and nothing.

I initially wanted to be alone but I met up with some of the Korean trainees, one of whom asked to accompany me. I was too polite and curious to say no. We went first to a convenience store where he insisted on buying me something to eat. I politely refused and we moved on to an internet cafe. I paid for this, which he did not like at all. It seemed to him that because I was in his country I was a guest and should pay for nothing. We walked around, visited a small island. I could not help noticing just how dirty the sea was, however.

[This Email from the Internet Cafe:]

Aneyonghaseo!

I am in Yeosu at the moment and in 24 hours, the ship will depart for the final leg to Yokohama. Thankyou for sending all the emails. I could not reply to them for several reasons, but no matter. I am keen to hear about Rose's exam progress and look forward to returning home. I now have the flight details so thankyou.

Klaas sends his regards as he leaves the ship to be replaced by Rob. Korea has been interesting and the trainees have been a real pleasure to work with. I have been keeping a detailed account to aid my memory.

Nick

Hiroshima

[The private journal of the voyage ends here, but Nick wrote for the Europa website again an account of the final leg to Japan.]

... the lasting memory of the Sail Korea event will be the friendliness and helpfulness of the trainees who have been on board. Even when times have been tough, their attitude has been superb and their spirits have never faded. On shore this does not change. We were once again treated to a traditional Korean meal, this time on board the ship, prepared by them. Yeosu was to be our last port of call before Japan and the meal was a fitting farewell. As we made ready for sea on the following day, we were joined by two new crewmembers, José from Spain and Yury from Vladivostok. Our number of trainees was down to only 4 for the next leg of the voyage, making the total crew smaller than it had been since the beginning of the event.

When sailing a tall ship, there are often moments of reflection. Sometimes these are inspired by something as simple as a sunrise or the impending arrival at a new destination. Our next port of call, Hiroshima in Japan, gave us much to fill these sheltered moments. Only 3 days since the ocean mists swallowed the Korean coast, we entered the city which has been etched into mankind's darkest chapters.

Many of the crew made the short walk from the dockyard to the museum and memorial park, which stands at the site which was once the hypocentre of an atomic explosion. It is an awesome yet wretched sight to gaze at the exact spot of sky where human history was distorted by the foulness of war. Directly below the hypocentre stands the scorched out remains of a hall now simply called the A-bomb dome. It will stand forever as a monument encircled by memory in its most tangible form. It is a moment captured by crumbling pillars and tortured metal, inspiring both sadness and hope for the future.

In the evening of the same day we resumed our journey to Yokohama as the last rays of sun dipped behind the coastal islands. In the days that followed we made our way through the islands of the Japanese archipelago. It was as if we were sailing through a city. Streets and shops could be seen on either side. We crossed under bridges and could hear the noise of traffic above. We were traffic ourselves. Freighters dart between islands, making the narrow stretches of water into highways. At night the lights of passing towns and cities silhouetted the yardarms and the eddy currents formed forked tongues of foam, licking at the side of the hull. We were an object from a bygone age, sliding through the ultra-modernity of urban Japan.

At the moment we are in open water. It is early morning, and the last traces of red sunlight are leaving the sky. The ship is garlanded in honour of Hans, our engineer's birthday. The air is warm but fresh as we cover the remaining distance to Yokohama.

[Nick left the ship for good in Yokohama and flew home. This poem must have been written soon after we drove home from Heathrow.]

Back in England

The moon marked time
The lamps were raining an orange sea
of gases and grime
in rancid waves to welcome me
The gloom that clustered in the neon light
The gloom worn in fashionable emptiness
Took to the air, and made a baby cry.
Paper shells like claws, kicked through old streets
An empty can, a bullet cartridge falls to ground
And all but one can hear that sound
The moon keeps time still, underneath a sea
And England spreads its streets to welcome me.

[Life moved on. The rest of the Pacific journal notebook is unceremoniously taken up with drafts for a pre-Oxford essay on Browning's 'The Ring and the Book'. However, a proprietorial feeling about *Europa* remained (he did two further short voyages aboard her in the remaining years) and it may be worth relating, personal though it is, that in November during his first term I emailed him as follows at his college, and got the most verbose email reply he ever sent:]

Hi Nick – I just logged on Europa website and the hot news is ... they have TIDIED OUT THE FOREPEAK! I quote –

'" ... disgorging years' worth of mummified paint, useless kindling, collected curiosities, and rusting thing-a-ma-jigs-all carried up a vertical ladder through a two-foot wide steel hatch and into the light of day. Like a flea market gone adrift, the raft of flotsam grew to cover the well deck, line both companionways, fill the interior of the deckhouse and swamp the entire main deck. Here was a mouth-watering smorgasbord for even the novice collector of random crap."'

Otherwise not much news here, went to do literary festival gigs in Bath and Wells, Rose starts Tesco next Monday, and my novel has AT LAST started to move forward without creaking with pain.

love MUM

[Reply from Nicholas]

Mother, I feel I should warn you that Europa's forepeak has what is always called the 'definitive tidy out' once every month. I have taken all the crap out of it, Glen has taken all the crap out of it, My friends John and Erika have taken all the crap out of it. I guarantee that right now, yes right now, the forepeak will somehow have reclaimed its old garage feeling and some apprentice will be planning to hold the 'definitive tidy out'.

I am glad about your novel coming along OK. If it goes quickly enough, you may soon be able to board Europa and instigate the 'definitive tidy out' in the forepeak.

Anyway, wish Rose luck in Tesco and tell her to wish me luck in Tennyson.

Yours artfully, Nick

OXFORD

[Nicholas went to Oxford in Autumn 2002. He was as passionately committed to poetry as ever, but the Pacific experience made him look back differently at his earlier desperation to get there. His prose energy having gone into essays, most of the personal writings from this time are poems.]

On Matriculation Day

The Dean takes his place in the opulent hall
Face rhinoceros grey.
We tune our ears for the Latin exchange.
The sun looks in
Without intention
Meaning as much
As a starter's gun
On 500 faces expecting to change

Such radiant hope on a meaningless stage
Forms the word 'Matriculation'

But not yet gone two years ago I cried
As if I was the less, being denied
The dreaming day of champagne mixed with pride.

Sunlight injured my eyes, the windows
gave an oceanic feel. The statues' robes
channelled the breeze outside
And rose and fell and fell
In the aftermath of a lifelong invitation
The words of which are simply 'Isolation ...'

At Poetry Society, First Term

Thursday readings, student Poetry
Parades its neurosis with pride
With wit, intangibly falling on me
Would it be rude to leave such seriousness?
Begin the war on boredom?
In my own room there is Anglo-Saxon.Here there is weariness.

'Shall we be friends who fuck?'
Such ingenious alliterations
Fill my fellows' publications
Such subjects seem to occupy
The heart or thereabout
Before young intellects hurl them out
In better rhyme than I

And soon they shall occupy my shelf
Maybe sometimes fall down on me
Prefaced with 'This one is about myself'

Well, this is me
My voice, my choice
To write what you will never see.
I fill the empty nights with words for fun
I am the rhythm shifter
And tonight I have only just begun.

Sanity

The sloppy warm half-foreign snacks
Enchant the 'Cafe Tear'
Before workrise, mind strikes eight
And Parker trickles in the ear.

D Phil D.S. Rolyne leans
All ring-eyed on the ring-marked desk,
Admires the faceless 'slut-cut' jeans
And bathes in half-excited rest.

Someone stands across the street
Half a loved one, half complete.
City, time and rhyme contract
Softening the coldness of concrete

A half-white light invades the street
And bodies march into the world
Away from lives which dreams have stirred
Into the paralysing sleet

Skies of orange, skies of grey
Like shifts of memory overlay
Eros and lethargy

Something underneath our feet
Is coming upwards day by day
The minstrel boys are on the run
They scud the sky
They scud the sky
What we were
We will become
As we add our heat
To the desert sun.

A Cold Night

The night sky won't connect
and the stars seem separated
in their rusty loops,
enchained in the half moon.
Stillness, not freshness
is captured in our passing faces.

The waterfalls have snapped
and are serrating
the cyclic nativity of a thousand roots.
They rise, devour earth and swoon
in the shivering light of the winter moon
enraptured , in our passing faces.

The frost left us cracked.
The air and the plane create
inapposite vastness, unrenewed.

To enervate, a small breeze croons,
'These nights are unproductive. Many moons

are written numbly on our passing face.'

Sheffield

The steel heart stops
The oak heart weeps
The workers flock
In bloody streets.

The steel heart stops
Time's silver shroud
In every clock
He will stand proud

The steel heart tears
The pure heart's bough
And carves concern
In every brow

The steel heart knocks
And drives the clocks
And in its veins
Stand office blocks.

86

I Saw You

I saw you again
In a pane of glass
When the evening glow was fading.
There you were,
reflecting me
twisting around my memory
tightening your grip on me.

I saw you again
In a pane of glass
when it started to rain
and the skies were masked
with grey disdain
mutinied the memory
and happiness breathes its last
and dullness quenched my pain.

Tighter and tighter
the circles you draw
until you are everywhere and everyone knew
I shan't look around
at sunsets and skies
My eyes sear the ground
As my happiness dies.

I Want

I want to fall
I want to fall
I want to become a glistening trail
As water swallows the evening sun
And I want the world to see
What the world has made of me

I want to fall like the sycamore
Distorting, winding trail
Sail on wings of failure
Dance in the sunbeam from above,
Mock and chant at the saints
Who hold the sun.
And gaze into the tepid pool
Of what I have become.

Stonefish

The sea thickens
In the coral dell
As the divers descend
Where the stonefish dwell

The light splits, in shafts
As the darkness swells
And creatures desert
The fatal well

Death eats colour
In a diving hell
dark since the time
that Man first fell

The stonefish are still
We are all alone
The stonefish are flesh
With heart of stone

The Sails of Time (Bored in the Bod)

Look into the mirror love
And see your blue eyes burning, burning
And think that in one mind my love
The blue fires burn on, yearning.

The colours that played swift around
The world while you were speaking
Have fallen, tarnished, to the ground
And strew around my grieving.

The silver sails sliced through the air
While twilight skies glowed with desire
But time's short course has dulled love's colours
And old visions are expiring
Visions are expiring

Light Pollution

The Sheldonian sky is orange
So is the Oxford night sky
But no cherub sits in the centre

Only If

If I feel love at all
it will take me to my grave
And if I have a soul
It will seek me in my cave

If I am a face in the crowd
I will burst like the rolling wave
And if I am allowed
I will foam into my tomb

On Michael Gearin-Tosh

[Note written for the Times 'Lives Remembered' on the death of Michael Gearin Tosh, senior lecturer in English at St Catherine's. Given the prevailing darkness of the poems, it is worth acknowledging clearly that Nicholas had, and recorded more informally, many moments of exaltation and satisfaction in the work he did at Oxford.]

When teaching, Michael would never leave a line of poetry un-interrogated, so a single poem or scene from a play could occupy us for two hours.

But at the end of one class he read, or rather performed, the whole of Browning's 'By the Fire Side' to us and announced; 'If that doesn't knock you for six then you have no business studying literature'.

It seems as if every text we studied with Michael became a favourite of mine, and this ability to illuminate the significance of detail in literature made him one of the most memorable teachers one could ever have.

The River

[Another major part of life at Oxford was the physical training attached to speed cycling and before that, to rowing (he rowed with the Oxford University lightweight squad). The only surviving rowing journal, unfortunately, is brief.]

... 30th.

Timed run: came 5th and strained my foot. This didn't affect the 50 minute erg I got given instead of an outing. God knows what Andy wants to see, but I think that I should be more aggressive. Well, to be honest I do know. 2:03.9 for 50 mins, so Fuck Up.

Poised at the catch, the blades arched in my hands
As once again I dropped them in the stream
And all along the beaten sheet, the sands
Were grey as cloud ...

3rd

The outing yesterday went well. It felt as if my blade would wash out when I drew level. Wallingford in the drizzle and early mist is even more hypnotic. The scenery doesn't change, just disappears into the grey. In a strange way it reminded me of sailing in the great Korean and Japanese sea mists, unable to see anything, just trapped in a tiny world until something else, a duck or another crew, comes into your bubble of life. The greens became grey, like the passing of the summer.

I feel as if my mind is adapting to the changes that must be made. A bit more mental muscle has been put on, replacing the summer fat.

Everyone seems more at ease with each other now, settling into the rhythm of things.

WEDS. The sky exploded, headachy over the river's coolness. A fisherman hooked the wing of a swan and its entire side was laid bare as, with one wing, it beat the water into foam. When the man reeled it in to remove the hook, he would be pecked and beaten, forced to let go again and again until with his virgin knife he sliced the twine. The wing would infect, but outside of his dreams, why should that bother him?

For a few moments, the river appeared to the sun from behind a cloud, so wherever the man looked it stared straight at him. It was in the sky, in the river, in the corner of his glasses and on the face of his watch. As a sculler slid past like a purposeful watersnake, it winked at him from one of the blades.

Not having caught anything all day, except the swan, he decided to leave the early November sunshine before it left him.

We do that, and our ripples are eating the riverbank, not as fast as the current though; and the sun is making the bank harder, although if the sun did not exist the river wouldn't evaporate, therefore there would be no rain to erode the bank. However, on a cold November day the river won't really be evaporating.

No, this rain is raised in the oceans, and this current by the rain and the moon, which will be eclipsed by the earth shadowing the sun tonight. But I won't see it, because of the cloud. Everything leads away from Man. So the world winds round the riverbend, and out of sight ...

A Forsaken Garden

[It is not within the scope of this collection to reproduce the many academic essays Nick wrote, but this short dissertation on a Swinburne poem is interesting as an example of his close-reading passion, and empathy for the 19th century vision.

As the poem is not especially well known, we reproduce it here first]

A Forsaken Garden
by Algernon Charles Swinburne

In a coign of a cliff between lowland and highland,
  At the sea-down's edge between windward and lee,
Walled round with rocks as an inland island,
  The ghost of a garden fronts the sea.
A girdle of brushwood and thorn encloses
  The steep square slope of the blossomless bed
Where the weeds that grew green from the graves of its roses
  Now lie dead.

The fields fall southward, abrupt and broken,
  To the low last edge of the long lone land.
If a step should sound or a word be spoken,
  Would a ghost not rise at the strange guest's hand?
So long have the gray bare walks lain guestless,
  Through branches and briars if a man make way,
He shall find no life but the sea-wind's restless
  Night and day.

The dense hard passage is blind and stifled
    That crawls by a track none turn to climb
To the strait waste place that the years have rifled
    Of all but the thorns that are touched not of time.
The thorns he spares when the rose is taken;
    The rocks are left when he wastes the plain.
The wind that wanders, the weeds wind-shaken,
    These remain.

Not a flower to be pressed of the foot that falls not;
    As the heart of a dead man the seed-plots are dry;
From the thicket of thorns whence the nightingale calls not,
    Could she call, there were never a rose to reply.
Over the meadows that blossom and wither
    Rings but the note of a sea-bird's song;
Only the sun and the rain come hither
    All year long.

The sun burns sear and the rain dishevels
    One gaunt bleak blossom of scentless breath.
Only the wind here hovers and revels
    In a round where life seems barren as death.
Here there was laughing of old, there was weeping,
    Haply, of lovers none ever will know,
Whose eyes went seaward a hundred sleeping
    Years ago.

Heart handfast in heart as they stood, 'Look thither,'
    Did he whisper? 'Look forth from the flowers to the sea;
For the foam-flowers endure when the rose-blossoms wither,
    And men that love lightly may die – but we?'
And the same wind sang, and the same waves whitened,
    And or ever the garden's last petals were shed,
In the lips that had whispered, the eyes that had lightened,
    Love was dead.

Or they loved their life through, and then went whither?
  And were one to the end – but what end who knows?
Love deep as the sea as a rose must wither,
  As the rose-red seaweed that mocks the rose.
Shall the dead take thought for the dead to love them?
  What love was ever as deep as a grave?
They are loveless now as the grass above them
  Or the wave.

All are at one now, roses and lovers,
  Not known of the cliffs and the fields and the sea.
Not a breath of the time that has been hovers
  In the air now soft with a summer to be.
Not a breath shall there sweeten the seasons hereafter
  Of the flowers or the lovers that laugh now or weep,
When as they that are free now of weeping and laughter
  We shall sleep.

Here death may deal not again for ever;
  Here change may come not till all change end.
From the graves they have made they shall rise up never,
  Who have left nought living to ravage and rend.
Earth, stones, and thorns of the wild ground growing,
  While the sun and the rain live, these shall be;
Till a last wind's breath upon all these blowing
  Roll the sea.

Till the slow sea rise, and the sheer cliff crumble,
  Till terrace and meadow the deep gulfs drink,
Till the strength of the waves of the high tides humble
  The fields that lessen, the rocks that shrink,
Here now in his triumph where all things falter,
  Stretched out on the spoils that his own hand spread,
As a god self-slain on his own strange altar,
  Death lies dead.

A Forsaken Garden

A Commentary

Underlying the rich yet stark profusion of imagery in *A Forsaken Garden* is a very clear philosophy on the nature of death and its relation to the way in which we live our lives. We begin in a realistic garden and are taken deep into the world of the metaphysical. Death becomes an essentially erotic figure because it satisfies itself by eliminating itself. Ideas of sexual intercourse and a lost love are subtly present throughout but most powerful is the starkness which is depressing yet utterly consuming.

> 'In a coign of the cliff between lowland and highland,
>   At the sea-down's edge between windward and lee,'

What is striking about these opening lines is the precision with which they encapsulate the mood and location of the preceding verses. 'between lowland and highland' and 'between windward and lee' together create a very obvious impression of the scene being in an indefinite and yet precise location. Later on the description of the wind playing around the garden explains the importance of it being between windward and lee. The implication from these lines is that it is half sheltered, which is a reflection on the half-death, half-life motif in the poem. The phrase 'the cliff' is mysterious since we have no idea exactly where Swinburne is at the time. We are forced to imagine our own cliff in order to compensate for our lack of knowledge. It is as if we have already been left behind and must catch up with the poet's stream of thought. Thus in these two words, he gains our attention and imaginative fixture. From the knowledge we have because of the title we must realise what an unlikely place for a garden the described location is.

> 'Walled round with rocks as an inland island,
>   The ghost of a garden fronts the sea.
> A girdle of brushwood and thorn encloses
>   The steep square slope of the blossomless bed
> Where the weeds that grew from the graves of its roses
>   Now lie dead.'

The third line of the first stanza serves to set this garden apart in its location from the images of vast generality which are called up by the word 'cliff'. 'The ghost of a garden' is an obscure yet inspiring image. Something more supernatural and emotional has been introduced into the poem and just as the first three lines concentrate and focus our imagination onto a specific garden and cliff, the fourth line sets it free to introduce vast notions of life, death and living death. The 'girdle of brushwood and thorn' is a sharper, less neutral image than that of rocks enclosing the garden because of the uncultivated sharpness which we associate with thorns. Furthermore, the image is narrowed down to the bed of soil within the ghostly garden. The steep slope of the blossomless bed strengthens the idea that the garden is being taken into the sea by erosion of the cliff. The final two lines of the stanza reflect the final lines of the poem in what they communicate about life and death. The weeds signify death for the roses and are now dead themselves. In all the verses, the final three syllable line is emphasised by its shortness and echo into the next verse. In this case a notion of death is set to overshadow the continuing physical description.

'The fields fall southward, abrupt and broken,
    To the low last edge of the long lone land.
If a step should sound or a word be spoken,
    Would a ghost not rise at the strange guest's hand?'

The process of a ghost rising is what happens in a way when Swinburne, or his character, recalls the lovers in the garden when they were alive. The fields falling southward is another literal image but one which connects with a more deathly decay of land falling into a consuming and infinite to the eye, sea.

'So long have the grey bare walks lain guestless,
    Through branches and briars if a man make way,
He shall find no life but the sea-wind's, restless
    Night and day.'

Here we become more aware of the presence of the poet in the poem itself. The grey bare walks lying guestless fits into the pattern of desolation which the poet has established but the idea that if any man makes his way into the garden suggests that the poet is either not in the garden and it is an entity which exists in imaginative memory or possibly that the narrator is a woman. The former seems to be more likely since the third line of the second verse suggests that if any word or step comes into the garden, a ghost would be raised. The Forsaken garden now becomes something deeply intertwined with memory and emotion, more profound than the mere mood established in the first stanza. The restlessness of the sea wind calls us back to the idea of the garden existing between windward and lee, half in and half out of shelter due to being in the coign of a cliff. The restlessness of the of the sea winds contrasts with the human emptiness of the garden.

'The dense hard passage is blind and stifled
  That crawls by a track none turn to climb
To the strait waste place that the years have rifled
  Of all but the thorns that are touched not of time.'

The 'dense hard passage' being blind and stifled is an image which builds on the paradox set up by the previous image of restlessness. A garden, especially a dead garden cannot be said to be restless and a passage, presumably formerly a traditional hedge-like garden passage cannot in itself be blind and stifled. Someone walking through it could be restless, blind and stifled and this would make the ascribed qualities transferred epithets. The fact that the poet claims that nobody is in the garden, and yet these epithets still apply give an even more ghostly and paradoxical feel to the poem. Because line 12 is in the form of a question we could also infer that the narrator has never been in the garden but has a form of omnipresence over the scene at this stage. Later on in the sixth stanza when a form of ghost is risen we could infer that the poet's presence has in fact raised the ghost of memory but the uncertainty of presence and absence, reflected in the repeated asking of questions forms the central paradox of the poem, as expressed in the closing lines.

The thorns being 'touched not of time' is a slightly unusual use of syntax, the function of which is to throw the word 'not' into emphasis above the word 'touched', a use which reflects the lack of time's ravages upon the thorns by the undermining of the role of 'touched' in the line. Although the thorn shrubs are technically weeds, which Swinburne claimed to be dead, the image is still an accurate and important one because the actual thorns themselves remain sharp, independent of the life of the plant. Therefore, what remains after death is the sharpness nurtured by the life which destroys, a central component of the poem's philosophy.

'The thorns he spares when the rose is taken;
  The rocks are left when he wastes the plain.
The wind that wanders, the weeds wind-shaken,
  These remain.'

Here the significance of the previous images of rocks and thorns is made more explicit. The remaining hardness and sharpness after life coincides with the unsatisfied souls which we associate with ghosts. What is giving the poet pain is not just the destruction of life but the fact that the destruction is incomplete just as a ghost represents incomplete death. The use of the word 'he' has the same mystical purpose as the word 'the' in line one. Who 'he' is is a mystery. As the poem develops we find out that he is death personified, as opposed to a conventional notion of God, as convention might lead us to believe.

'Not a flower to be pressed of the foot that falls not;
    As the heart of a dead man the seed-plots are dry;
From the thicket of thorns whence the nightingale calls not,
    Could she call, there were never a rose to reply.
Over the meadows that blossom and wither
    Rings but the note of a sea-bird's song;
Only the sun and the rain come hither
    All year long.'

The extreme negativity in this stanza purposely suspends the steady progression of the poet from his beginning to conclusion. The absence of life in the garden is emphasised, in a way unnecessarily in terms of the poem's central argument. The purpose of it is to show a melancholic slowing of spirit, a contemplation of how deprived of life the garden is. The lack of response to an absent nightingales sweetness and the lack of flowers for feet to crush works up an idea of how dependant upon other life one life is to give it its natural sweetness, hence we begin to see the importance of lovers in nature, as the next stanza shows us.

'The sun burns sere and the rain dishevels
    One gaunt bleak blossom of scentless breath.
Only the wind here hovers and revels
    In a round where life seems barren as death.'

Life seeming barren as death is an important and powerful line in the poem. The unity formed between life and death in this phrase helps us to view the paradox of presence and absence for the narrator. Swinburne is able to assume a present absence because, as we have seen in the previous stanza, life is something in which many lives must participate, all that remains else is barren and dead. The single gaunt bleak blossom seems born to die and therefore its life is a form of death, a concept which we quickly extrapolate to include the human condition.

'Here there was laughing of old, there was weeping,
    Haply, of lovers none ever will know,
Whose eyes went seaward a hundred sleeping
    Years ago.'

What we have inferred about the reciprocal nature of life from the previous images is made explicit here when the poem turns to love and physical as well as emotional life returns to the poem in the form of conjectural memory. The hundred sleeping years appears to be simply an expression rather than referring to a specific date and has the function of casting the mind back in time, mentally bringing life to the scene. The reference to eyes going seaward is the one phrase in these lines which casts our mind back to the previous implications of the sea gradually making barren and consuming the land, like a force of death.

'Heart handfast in heart as they stood, 'Look thither,'
    Did he whisper? 'look forth from the flowers to the sea;
For the foam-flowers endure when the rose-blossoms wither,
    And men that love lightly may die – but we?

Here we have the first example of naivety being portrayed in the poem. The foam – flowers are what will eventually begin to consume the garden and are an effect of the unchanging wind which will play about the garden when it is dead. The lovers are effectively looking out from the mortality represented by the garden to immortality represented by the sea but not understanding that the function of the unchanging is not to preserve but to destroy, that its constancy will destroy them.

'And the same wind sang and the same waves whitened,
    And or ever the garden's last petals were shed,
In the lips that had whispered, the eyes that had lightened,
    Love was dead.'

The constancy of the wind and waves is iterated. The phrase 'Love was dead' is connected through the rhyme to the shedding of petals and takes us back to the constant present of the poet. Two lovers were our the invocation for the leap back in time and what is best described as the re-death of love and emotion takes us back to the dead garden so that we may be further depressed by Swinburne.

'Or they loved their life through, and then went whither?
    And were one to the end – but what end who knows?
Love deep as the sea as a rose must wither,
    As the rose-red seaweed that mocks the rose.
Shall the dead take thought for the dead to love them?
    What love was ever as deep as a grave?
They are loveless now as the grass above them
    Or the wave.'

The first line of the stanza builds up a notion of hope and after the caesura, destroys it with a question which reflects the bleak vastness of the destructive sea. The profusion of questions being asked shows the utter hopelessness of any answer which they might yield. Since the narratorial position is so obscure the questions are more flung out into the darkness than flung at us. They are questions which have been answered by the preceding poem and drive in the knife of mortality for the reader. The idea being expressed is that however deep love is, it must fade while the forces of death and destruction do not. The image of red seaweed mocking the rose builds develops a mirror notion between life and death. Love may be as deep as the sea and roses redder than the seaweed but the former decays while the latter continues in its course. The final line, 'or the wave' reasserts the difference between the 'foam flowers' and the roses which the naive lovers compared.

'All are at one now, roses and lovers,
  Not known of the cliffs and the fields and the sea.
Not a breath of the time that has been hovers
  In the air now soft with the summer to be.'

The phrase 'all are at one now' is important in helping us to remember the discriminations which the poet is and is not making. Death has normalised the roses and lovers, to what exactly remains unclear and indeed un-implied. The poet is not concerned with an afterlife as such but with the unchanging forces of destruction which unify all life in death. What is important is that old life is at one, whether at peace or not is irrelevant to the particular focus of the poem. Their irradiation is made clear by the lack of impression which they made on history. The coming summer would conventionally be an image of relief but we know from earlier that the sun is something which burns and brings no solace to us, wrapped up as we are in Swinburne's reality. The next four lines of the stanza reflect the last four in that they project the same principle into the future reminding, as if it is necessary, the reader that they will undergo the same process. Although the narrator has an omnipresent air about the garden, he is not exempt from this fate.

'Here death may deal not again for ever;
  Here change may come not till all change end.
From the graves they have made they shall rise up never,
  Who have left nought living to ravage and rend.
Earth, stones, and thorns of the wild ground growing,
  While the sun and the rain live, these shall be;
Till a last wind's breath upon all these blowing
  Roll the sea.'

Our interest cannot but be stimulated by the idea of death being unable to recur when we compare it to the message of the preceding verses. From the final line of the previous stanza 'We shall sleep' we gather that the place being referred to is the plain of death so it is not an uplift of spirits which we experience when we read this line but with a sense of paradoxical irony that being dead, we cannot be killed again. The image of rolling the sea in the final line is the most powerfully active and immense one used in the poem up to this point. We get the impression of the sea being rolled up onto the land and thus engulfing it. Because the sea is so closely related to destruction we see that this image is in fact apocalyptic.

The final verse is fittingly where the two opposing notions of life and death which form the central paradox underlying the poem are brought together into a philosophical unity. We have seen throughout the poem a very clear philosophical direction being expressed through the richness of the imagery. The first four lines of the stanza continue the apocalyptic note set up in the penultimate stanza. The closing lines make clear the poet's conception of death.

'Here now in his triumph where all things falter,
    Stretched out on the spoils that his own hand spread,
As a god self-slain on his own strange altar,
    Death lies dead.'

Death seeks destruction and therefore when its goal is achieved in full it no longer has a role. The image of an altar compliments the ghostly mysticism which has run through the poem. The lower case g in god reminds us that it is not a christian god to which the poet is referring. The pagan or ancient implication has a certain primal appeal, as if time has completed its cycle at the end of the poem and what remains are the ancient principles and concepts which formed the world.

TROUBLED

~⁓~

[What follows is found in notebooks, dates uncertain, between 2004 and 2006. He completed his finals, although during this period he suffered a great deal of mental distortion, well-concealed; for postgraduate research on Imagist poetry he went to Liverpool University to do a PhD, dropping out after a term and a half as his illness progressed.]

The soul is the river which flows along a valley, into which the rivers of good and evil run. The human soul does not only represent the meeting of good and evil, but its unity and solution.

If God exists, he is the sun, casting not only light but shadow into this valley. The uncontrollably dark gulleys and caves through which the river must run are the darker regions of the soul, as much a result of God's presence as the light.

When asking God to shine on us, we must accept the shadows cast upon our own souls. God knows that the human soul is the unity of good and evil, that our faults are intrinsic to us, just as our good points are. I fully accept that I am the battlefield for Heaven and Hell more than most. I seek not for resolution, since I am the resolution.

… I have become the human battlefield for good and evil. Demonic insanity forces me to fetter my will to write my narrative, to follow its silver and delicate thread back into the world of shape, relation and meaning. But every time the wave of nightmare carries me on, and I lose touch with the slender thread of reality, washed away into the land of the walking dead, unable to share and dying along 10,000 times a day, waiting for a kind soul to unshackle me from this world.

[He began to write in the third person, detachedly, during the final year's crisis.]

The Private Document

He looked through the clumsy drawer full of his old writings, pausing on a poem about a girl, which badly expressed so many

101

things he no longer felt. The blandness of the whole thing was evident to his now urbanised sensibilities, but the fact that he had written it returned the memory of lying in the old bunk, the intensity of heat and the motion of the ship heightening those thoughts and causing the writing to become odd, not like his usual, compact style. If he was hailed as a genius and his work published in many languages, in many different books and typefaces, the oddness, the newness of that skewed writing would be cast into oblivion, that record of the ship's every lurch, the overture to his stupid crush would be lost.

Better to throw this one away, keep it perfect. But he had written it, he had felt it once and only he could remember the blazing moments in which friendship had turned to affection and (was it love? Of course not). Conversations until dawn, the first he had ever had with a girl (she had been a woman, he a boy, he reflected) and a spirit being born which lonely years had almost negated. The uneven lines of poetry said nothing of this growth, nothing of the memories that lay behind it. He was the only one for whom the scrap of paper would live, it was a dead thing in the austere poetic universe but in its crumpled curvature he could perceive a sail, furled in his drawer but now straining with the life of his former self.

He tried to write poetry in Oxford, he even reflected on the fact that when ...... (he would look the name up later) had painted the roof of the Sheldonian, that the cherubic shades of orange would later fill the real sky as a result of light pollution, with the notable abscence of cherubs.

He was not a poet. The poetry society meetings left him with a feeling of admiration for the poets and an equal and opposite feeling of emptiness inside himself where he felt poetic ideas were failing to form. He found a formula for writing essays and when they became complacent, his tutors would jump on him. Not without a fight, the spirit which had been born in the Pacific trade winds dwindled and the bad private documents were replaced by analytical typeface which, even when he looked at them now, with a more developed eye, had nothing beyond themselves to say to him.

He never studied prose, prose always seemed too crushingly complete. Three years of studying poetic intensity passed, inspiring, stimulating, but not intense or poetic in themselves, except for those brief moments when the radio fell silent and thought filled the terrible arena of his mind.

He returned to the ship for a brief period between M.A. and B.A., the period which he now occupies. There was one person who he had hoped to see and who was, of course, absent. To the dispassionate eye the relatively innocent relationship he experienced would be easily dismissed, but he doesn't have the emotional equipment to do this. Instead he alternates between the unfeeling complacency of his former self and the burning thought that there was a connection spanning distance, years and superficial differences, a thought which stops him from sleeping and pins him to the pillow in the mornings.

He has been honest, he does not care who laughs at his thoughts, his introspections, his apologies.

... After accepting his lack of talent for life, he began to think about being put to sleep. Not like an animal but literally put to sleep until it was time to die. He would wake up, say something profound, then death (which is nothing at all like sleep, you just have your eyes closed for both).

As it was he woke up daily to see sunlight breaking through the curtains, an effect which destroyed the fantasies of the formless shapes of his dreams, or the sky might be grey. Either way, he would wake up, no further along the non-existent journey of life promoted by the world at large.

Biography made a story where there was no story, 'I left this and got a job in that' etc. Seldom did any of the authors mention the weeks when nothing occurred.

No fear

I'm afraid of nothing,
I am afraid of the vast, indifferent nothing that,
on waking when its dark,
I know hell to be composed of.

In the street
The eyes about me do not turn
And when I do not turn '

A haiku

Pounding round poems
Wasn't very good for you.
Zeig heil! mister Pound

I like the slash at the end of web addresses. It offers perpetually greater specificity of all websites. It offers a small sense of endlessness/

Tate Liverpool

If this is art, then art
Is everywhere and everything.
metal is a soul.
paint is fear on the wall.

Castle

The icy castle stands among the stars
Above the clinging dew and hanging mists.
It sways and buckles in celestial breeze
Like melting icicles, engulfed in surging seas.

Now hear the gushing, wailing waterfalls
The crystal trails that dance to worlds below
And leave their echoes in the corridors
And cut the icy stones in shadow floes.
The circles of a thousand dying screams
Resound again in corridors of dreams.

So in a dream I did ascend the tower
And saw dark poems spread like tapestries
They sang with voices of infinity
Like stars reflected in a glassy sea
They sang to angels captured in the sky
And for a moment, brief, they sang to me.

BLAST AGAINST THE CRITICS, 2006

[During his postgraduate time in Liverpool University, there were more confident moments, and in an uncharacteristically combative mood Nicholas produced one of the few pieces of deliberate journalism of his life, and was considering submitting it for publication, so strong was his view of the wrong turn his subject was taking.]

How do you justify literary criticism as an industry? I recently found myself trying to explain to a chemistry graduate that I had opted to stay at university for a few more years, paying vast amounts of (my parents') money to continue studying poetry. This involves looking up dates of composition, printing practices, reading obscure letters and so on. This chemist was an eloquent person but could only remark 'sounds a bit boring'. He was wrong. It is mind-numbingly boring, and it probably won't cure cancer either. I spend my life reading other people's essays in journals in abject fear of studying an already 'overworked' area, petrified that my thesis will be invalid.

If you haven't encountered one before, a literary journal contains seven or eight articles of about eight thousand words. Hundreds of these are produced every year and have to be stored in book-stacks, large rooms with bookshelves that are wound along on rails, so that more journals can be packed in. These publications are not intended for public enjoyment but only for scholars, for those people who wish to add one more article to the millions in existence and need other articles to refer to. Going into an ordinary bookshop will simply not highlight just how many thousands of acres there is of this stuff, it's mind-blowing.

Back to my chemist in the pub ... 'Sounds a bit like history' he commented. This made me feel a little better as literary history sounds cultural and scientific, less flimsy than being a literary critic. However, I'm not a historian and neither are most of the journal-ists. People who only study literature generally become pseudo-historians or pseudo-psychologists, imitators of the analytical mode they feel they can apply. I am acutely aware that after three years of study I am expert at nothing. I voiced my concerns about the whole thing to an old tutor of mine, someone who I have great respect for. He said that if either he or his colleagues thought about the mass of other criticism the whole time they would go mad. It is one of the paradoxes of the critical industry that while it embraces intellectual solidarity in its works, it must perform an act of doublethink in order to believe that what it produces is necessary in any way.

There are a few good critics like John Carey, Valentine Cunningham and Duncan Wu. Hermione Lee's biography of Virginia Woolf got me genuinely interested in her life and works (something which Virginia Woolf was unable to do). However, for every good academic there are probably a hundred awful ones in universities across the globe from Luton to Alabama. It's not that literature shouldn't be studied at all but my proposal is that it is left to non-literary specialists, the people who could bring qualified and original perspectives to art. I'm calling for people like myself to be banned from books until they get some real qualifications. Too much bad writing has been written about good writing and it is ruining English as a subject, reducing it to a weird network of theory. The practice of published criticism has been around since before the time of Alexander Pope. It is time to stop accepting it.

Literature is often flamboyant and frivolous and should be written about in such a way. Instead, the world of literary academia is ruled by uninspired, New Labour-type, Hazel Blears-esque, natural born administrators and vain products of the Thatcher years. There is no more need to acknowledge these pedants than there is need to acknowledge the dress-sense of the 1970s when I put on clothes.

A good writer can learn more from looking out of the window than some can by travelling the world.

THE SILENCE AT THE SONG'S END

[Nicholas left Liverpool in early 2006, resolved to get a job in the outside world. He had a happy fortnight at the National Theatre, working in the director's office and helping with outside projects with reportedly great enthusiasm: 'gentle, kind and wonderfully intelligent, he embraced any assignment with interest and care', they wrote after his death.

He did a week at a publisher's and a week in *The Times*, also with glowing reports. One colleague wrote: 'a really bright, sweet boy, who wasn't fazed by having to come up with ideas on the spot in features meetings, or being dragged off to Buckingham Palace to doorstep old ladies who'd been to the Queen's birthday lunch. He was quiet and thoughtful but also smiley and keen, giving no hint of finding life a challenge.'

He considered journalism, but only briefly.]

Journalism

To be a journalist everybody says you need an angle on events. I can't honestly say that I can grasp this concept. Certainly, you have to interpret fact in your own way, as everybody always does. Life is surely an infinite series of interpretations of objects and actions.

The difference with journalism must be that it is both a portrayal of the object itself, and a guide to how it may or should be interpreted. If a child has been killed, a journalist will convey this fact, although the reader will probably be aware of the fact that a child is dead. The function of the journalist maybe to re-convey the fact, viewing it in context or isolation or from one political standpoint or another.

I would have to ask a journalist, but it seems to me that a successful article is one which deepens retrospect, which adds humanity to fact, making it true in a greater sense. For example, the death of this child will be blamed on the parents, the poor supervision at school, the upbringing of the murderer or alcohol intake of the driver. A journalist can effectively act as the historian of the present, much like the Anglo-Saxon poets, when poetry was news.

Qwerty

why is the y
next to the t?
I guess
You're in luck
If you want to
write 'I am a guy
With a gut.'

[Nicholas' wit, courtesy and obliging gentleness remained intact, as far as those around him were concerned, right up to the day of his death. Indeed even within the final months he had some genuinely happy moments, particularly in the high Colorado Rockies in January; he also showed great friendship and kindness towards a young girl from a troubled background who came, rather shyly, to stay with us a couple of times. Even within his last week, he put himself out to be hospitable towards her, just as he had to the young Koreans on the ship three years earlier.

However, the demons had returned during the early summer, bringing the work placements to an end with a violent attack of depression mingled with terrifying delusions. These are recorded in a last notebook but in his life were kept severely hidden, although he saw two psychiatrists and a very supportive GP on numerous occasions during his last month. He denied that he was suicidal, and it is plain from the last, unpublished notebook that he resisted the opportunity and impulse strongly on at least one occasion.

He began to show signs of improvement and to plan an entirely new career, taking a low-paid job as a classroom assistant in London and studying in the evenings at Birkbeck College, to begin the long training of a Jungian psychotherapist. The attacks, delusions and nightmare miseries, however, returned, and it became apparent to those of us near him that he was fighting for control against something beyond any ordinary depression. He fought it bravely, exhausting himself with long runs and refusing to take even a glass of wine with his supper; but he absented himself to his room more and more. The final, largely incoherent and unhappy nocturnal diary is not something to publish; apart from a few fragments which relate to his earlier perception and writings.]

The May Field

The spring seemed to come late, and April had resembled February in its monstrous greyness, sucking the colour away from the earth. It had been my habit to wake up naturally with the light every morning but on most days it had scarcely arrived and I awoke close to midday knowing that soon I would be tired again. Now, on the other hand, the weather has a spring-like vitality and I see the showers and cloud shadows sweep across the fields from the window of my study. In retrospect I suppose I should have remained in Micronesia where I was in touch with the world, anywhere but here, in touch with nature or rather, every nature except human.

Her

For Her, the world must be in order
Her concepts line up row by row,
Her universe has a well-drawn border,
A pond for effect, and art nouveau.

Tower Bridge has left the Universe
Its own sides have swung open and it passes, ship-like, through itself into oblivion

I was trying to escape the excessively cerebral lifestyle,
but there is no escape. Alone or in company, thoughts, useless thoughts continually swirl around, producing nothing, using energy with no output, an impossibility in physics.

Personality means your chosen mask, or maybe your involuntary outward show. It can be treated. I am socially palatable, there is no disorder. It is my soul that is sick, so I exercise the awful right to perpetual internal misery. Does believing that I am sick make me more sick or less sick?

[Sometime in the small hours of Monday 26th June, Nicholas took his life. Despite the shock and sadness for us, the atmosphere in the quiet garden-room where he lived and kept his beloved library was markedly peaceful. A struggle, which despite his considerate self-control had been felt like a hostile force-field around him for weeks, was over.

The papers and notebooks which make up this book were discovered gradually over the two following months, and have been transcribed unaltered. But one of the first passages to fall under my hand in that room, on that morning, was from a notebook filled four years before, when he was only 19. This is what Nicholas wrote, and was among the texts we sent to the many who mourned him.

It is wholly typical of him in its strangeness, its love for humanity and its sense that the mysteries of life are best approached through great art; and that art itself is not a parlour game but a key to truth.]

Every life is a tragedy. Our end is inevitable from the very moment that our characters emerge, and the thrill of the thing is not in the end itself but in the route we take to reaching that end. Since I am the main character, anything anyone knows about me acts as the chorus, providing the balance in order for my character to be established and contrasted.

The notion of life as a tragedy is not one which should be taken in a negative sense. Far from it. Our lives represent, in the words of Milton, the highest form of Drama. Our deaths do not so much represent the end of our character as the completion of our character. There is nothing more to know about ourselves but that the tragic formula is complete. It is the perfect moment which one may call heaven.

The fact of the matter is, the people to whom we refer as lowlifes and consider to be below us, are not excluded from a tragic experience equally great to that of Aristotle or Milton. All life is one, and he who watches another man's tragedy will gain the equivalent of the highest literary enlightenment. Inequality of expression is not inequality of mind.

[Later, we found what seems to be his last complete poem. It was read aloud by the bo'sun on the deck of the sailing-barque *Europa* on a calm evening in August, halfway up the Bay of Biscay. Captain Rob Vos and some of his Pacific and Atlantic shipmates joined his parents in giving Nick's ashes to the sea and repeating his words.]

The morning runs
on, a springtime secret
through the avenues
and avenues which lure
all sound away

I sing, as I was taught
inside myself.
I sing inside myself
when wild moments
slice some tender evening
like a breeze
that rattles gravel
and digs in the dirt

I sing, as I was told,
inside myself.
I sing inside myself
the one wild song, song that whirls
my words around
until a world unfurls

my ship's new sail
I catch the dew and set
a course amongst the ocean curls

The silence at the song's end
Before the next
Is the world

[We scattered the ashes in the middle of a Tall Ships race, from the ship he had loved best. Afterwards, his father Paul Heiney described the moment:]

'We had two very rough days after leaving Spain – big waves, heavy swell – and made very slow progress northwards so that after four days we were only half way across the Bay of Biscay.

On Monday the 14th the weather eased, the wind fell away and the sea flattened. The mood on board *Europa* lightened and those who had so far not dared to come on deck braved themselves for a first sight of the sea. The skipper, Rob Vos, who sailed with Nick in the Pacific, suggested that this might be a suitable night to sprinkle the ashes.

By evening the wind had died completely and the sea was flat. For the first time it felt warm. There was an undeniable sense of calm after the storm embracing the ship. The iPods came out, and after supper the deck saloon rattled to rap played over loudspeakers. There was laughter, clinking of glasses, giggling. It was party time.

At nine o'clock half a dozen of us arranged to meet on the stern deck – just those who knew Nick and had sailed with him including Rensje, the cook, who adored him. It felt a bit uncomfortable at first, no one quite certain how to feel or behave.

So I said, "Let's try not to be sad. Nick had some of the best days of his life sailing in this ship, and now he sails with you forever." Libby said how much he had loved working on the ship, and that some of his seizings and splices were still up in the rigging, keeping the crew safe as he had meant them to. Rob read out a list of all the voyages Nick had been on. The Bo'sun read the poem.

I unscrewed the lid of the plastic pot and gently sprinkled his ashes to and fro into the sea. The ship was perfectly still, not moving so much as an inch through the water.

Nick's ashes fell very lightly and formed a wide mat around the stern of the ship. Had there been the slightest breeze they would have been taken by it, but the air was so still that they tumbled like a mist and seemed to cling to *Europa* for a while. Very slowly, the ashes started to sink, and because of the clarity of the water we watched them for some while as they made their way deep into the ocean, a paleness in the blue water. Rob brought out a bottle of wine and we drank to Nick's memory as the sun set.

Then, a few minutes after the ashes had disappeared, we noticed that the surface of the sea became agitated, as it does when ruffled by a breeze. But there was not a breath. The ruffling of the water spread in a large circle around the ship and we debated for some time if it could be the effect of tide or current, but nobody came up with a convincing answer. Beyond the ripple we could see still, calm water, but for fifteen minutes the sea around *Europa* poppled as if being stirred by a breeze we could not feel. Then a real breeze appeared and the ship inched ahead through the water. We noted the position from the GPS – his ashes were scattered at 46.16N, 7.12W.

The breeze did not last and the ship was totally becalmed all night to the extent that the following morning she was in more or less the same position. The light went, but a mist hung round the horizon, blurring the world until you looked overhead, any time that night, and saw the moon and stars with contrasting clarity. We still drifted; in the hours after the ashes, *Europa* hardly left the spot. For the first time in the voyage, the ship stayed awake all evening, none of the crew or young trainees seeming to need their sleep as much as in the preceding days. The deckhouse beneath our quiet spot on the poop-deck rang with talk and laughter until late.

Next morning there was a beautiful sunrise. Later in the day, our first and only fair wind of the voyage sprang up, and the ship moved on. There were dolphins, the first we had seen all trip'.

AFTERWORD

by Professor Duncan Wu, St Catherine's College Oxford

This is the testament of a remarkable young man. As his tutor, I first came to know Nick Heiney as an alert, highly sensitive reader of poetry – acutely responsive to the nuances of words. It is a gift in which Nick was peculiarly blessed. He was at his happiest when, in tutorials, he spoke at leisure on the pantheism of Wordsworth and Coleridge or the beliefs of Herbert and Vaughan.

I remember a tutorial, in the summer term of 2004, during which I refrained from asking about the literary preoccupations of the previous week, instead enquiring about his experiences with the crew of the *Europa*. He spoke with unwonted confidence about the minutiae of life on board ship as I listened, prompting him from time to time as he elaborated on what it was to be in the middle of the ocean, in charge of a boat. This was not the kind of student into whose mind one poured knowledge; he tutored you.

From then onwards I was aware that he experienced certain things with the intensity of a Romantic, something I would have realised sooner had I read the journals and notes that make up this narrative. It is no accident that one of Nick's favourite poems was Shelley's 'Alastor' – the story of a poet who, bewitched by the spirit of solitude, is drawn further and further into a dark, unknowable vortex. Although the journey described in this volume is distinctively his, it parallels that of Shelley's unnamed protagonist. Nick seems to have figured his own life through the prism of that poem, and it provides the mythic core around which his journal is shaped.

There is nothing contrived about that. It happens, quite simply, to be how Nick saw his life, something underwritten by the honesty with which he writes. He describes what he sees as straightforwardly as he can, depicting his own motives and conduct with scrupulous fidelity to the moment. There was a moral imperative to tell the truth, which permeates his writing.

For that reason he paints an astonishingly accurate portrait of himself. Those who knew him remember his generosity of spirit, the quality Wordsworth means when he writes of 'little unremembered acts of kindness and of love'. That is to say, there was nothing premeditated or calculated in it. Some might have looked down on the young Koreans who joined the crew of the *Europa*, but his first thought is to make them as welcome as he can, remembering 'how welcome I was made'. Helping one of them to man the rigging, he notes his inability to step onto the course yard, but admires 'the way in which he endeavoured to do so'. Some days later he takes another Korean up to unfurl the royal: 'She had never climbed so high before and to my mind showed extreme gallantry in what cannot have seemed an easy task.' He would have made a good teacher.

One is aware constantly of Nick's observant, perceiving consciousness as it monitors the ebbs and flows of his own mood. He can be painfully self-analytical, most obviously when he speaks of depression and 'future madness' – but makes it his business to record such things with accuracy. There are times when he avoids the company of others, quite deliberately, and others when he is brutally hard on himself, as when he wonders whether he will be able to sleep after being berated for 'something which I had sometime done something wrong with'. He is sensitive almost to a preternatural degree about other people and things – aware for instance of the strange sense in which the *Europa* is instinct with life, dependent for its existence on the care and conscientiousness of those on board. It is part of what he calls the 'romanticism of the ship', and it is what makes the description of his visit to Nonwin Atoll so haunting – the eye of the storm, a strange, primeval interlude.

Nick was as aware as anyone of the truthfulness of great writing, and there are quotations throughout his diary from the poets he loved – Eliot, Keats, Herbert. And yet his voice in these pages is seldom other than clear, well-defined, mature, as if he has been writing for years. There is no posturing, no sentimentality, and no self-flattery. He speaks of what he sees, and always tells the truth.

These are just some of the qualities that make Nick's story much more than a mere act of self-expression. He didn't fool himself, and perhaps wasn't capable of it. That may go some way towards explaining why he ended his life as he did. But he left behind a written record of his journey into the vortex. It is a powerful piece of writing, exemplary in its sanity and clear-sightedness.

Ascott-under-Wychwood,
September 2006

... And a Final Word

by Rose Heiney

The work that you have just read depicts a vivid inner life. It conjures a mystic, a poet, a troubled man granted a tiny glimpse through the doors of perception. It's a wonderful document and I, more than anyone, am glad that it exists. It's a remarkable testament to a remarkable man. Yet there is always more to say, and I'd like to have a little go at telling you about the outer Nick; the face presented to the world, and the one that I knew.

I spent over twenty years in the company of a truly top-class brother. Throughout this time, I was largely unaware of his rare depth and insight. I didn't know quite how deep his affinity for poetry ran. All this writing, discovered after his death, is something of a shock to me. Although Nick and I were both English Literature students, our paths through the canon couldn't have been more different. As Nick spent his undergraduate days plunging boldly into Wordsworth, scaling Blakeian heights and hurling himself at any Milton he could find, I chuckled over Edward Lear and turned out droll little essays on Rattigan. Nick spent his nights wrestling with 'The Ring and the Book', I spent mine passed out with a kebab on my chest. No-one ever seemed to believe that we were brother and sister.

This bothered me. I was proud of him, and I wanted to introduce him to people. Because for all his diffidence, his shyness, and his discomfort, he was a pleasure. On the most basic, mundane, earthly, pizza-munching level he was lovely to have around. He was always fragile, always uneasy, often seemingly on the verge of leaving the room. But whenever he stuck around, he was welcome.

He was a remarkably generous conversationalist; gentle, focused, and interested. He was also a remarkably generous laugher. It never took much to move him to a few seconds of genuine mirth, and his laugh was a treat; a moment of awkward abandonment, a tense but broad smile, and an absolute engagement with whatever had amused him. My best memories of Nick revolve around sitcom; meeting at six o'clock to watch *The Simpsons*, then again at ten for *Frasier*, sometimes sitting up late together to hammer through a series of *Peep Show* or *Black Books*. Alone in his room, he listened to BBC 7 and watched Bill

Hicks DVDs, the next morning relaying to us the funniest lines he'd heard during the night. My Christmas present (he was the most thoughtful gift-buyer you could ever hope to meet) was generally some comedy – Bill Bailey, Dylan Moran, more *Frasier* – and a massive bar of cheap chocolate to eat whilst watching it.

He had a taste for theatre, often big, daft, splashy theatre; *Jerry Springer: The Opera, Donkeys' Years, The Producers*. He came loyally to watch me perform in ropey student comedy shows, always laughing where appropriate and sending a characteristically polite e-mail afterwards. He was, perhaps, the perfect audience for light entertainment : he watched and listened without cynicism or side, looking for the best in whatever he was seeing. Whether it was *Love, Actually* or the darkest, most surreal late-night radio rant, he would always find something to enjoy.

I suppose what I'm driving at here is that Nicholas was not a detached Romantic, standing in a Hebridean wilderness gazing upon the light and shadow of eternity. He enjoyed, for a long time, many of the dafter aspects of the world. He had time and relish for gleeful idiocy and junk food. He was brilliant – brilliant ! – at assembling fajitas.

And he himself was funny. He had a peculiar affinity with our family cat, an obese black moggy, and I'll never forget the sight of a fully adult Nick adorning said cat with a gold medallion and pointing out, correctly, how much he looked like Barry White. Or when he climbed into our Mum's much-mocked VW Beetle convertible – the back seats of which were generally strewn with two hundred pairs of socks, some crushed Maltesers, and a Nautical Almanac – and observing 'Little Noddy would never have left his car in such a state.' When Liverpool was mentioned as a possible place for him to do his Master's Degree he responded, deadpan as ever, 'Liverpool? I thought that was just a Crown Court , where Relatives Broke Down.'

Nicholas was very, very good company. Quiet, but whenever he spoke it would be worth the wait. As I yammered on pointlessly, giving my views on anything and everything and thinking that I was the most amusing person in the whole world, Nick would sit silently, then eventually chime in with something brilliant; pithy and astute. On numerous family holidays I shared rooms and boats and tents with him, and never once wished that I was with anyone else. His vulnerability spared us the usual sibling rivalry; it was just nice to see him happy.

I remember when he came back from his trip aboard Europa, fit, tanned, experienced and sick-makingly gorgeous. He'd just been to visit our old school for Speech Day, and girls had fallen like ninepins in their admiration of his new physical beauty. He stood in the garden, alone, with the family dog at his feet. I looked at him and decided then that I had the coolest, most brilliant big brother that I could ever have hoped for. I stand by that decision.

So even if Nicholas had written nothing, even if he hadn't left us such fantastic evidence of his inner life, I wouldn't mind. I loved the other side of him, the everyday Nick who was just as real and valid as Nick the diarist. I am uniquely privileged to have memories of him sitting on the sofa, looking strangely regal in his patterned dressing-gown, laughing at The *Simpsons* and feeding prawn crackers to the cat. That, for me, is enough.

Suffolk,
November 2006